GRADUATE RESEARCH

a guide for students in the sciences

GRADUATE RESEARCH

a guide for students in the sciences

ROBERT V. SMITH

Philadelphia

Published by

 A Subsidiary of the
Institute for Scientific Information®
3501 Market St., University City Science Center, Philadelphia, PA 19104 U.S.A.

Library of Congress Cataloging in Publication Data

Smith, Robert V., 1942–
  Graduate research.

  Bibliography: p.
  Includes index.
  1. Research—Methodology. I. Title.
Q180.55.M4S58 1984   507′.2   84-15711
ISBN 0-89495-037-1
ISBN 0-89495-038-X (pbk.)

Printed in the United States of America
90 89 88 87 86 85 84   8 7 6 5 4 3 2 1

To my mother and father

Contents

Preface

. . . in a scientific laboratory, nothing startling
which calls for an obvious response occurs on
its own. Nature is passive and silent. Scientists
have to start things up for themselves.
                    —JUNE GOODFIELD

Research and scholarship are the lifeblood of a technological society. Professional people in many different fields at one time or another will have to conduct research; thus, it is crucial for graduate students in the sciences to master this skill. Their advanced degrees depend upon it.

A worrisome paradox lurks in graduate education. At this level, more than at any other, the student must develop independence and creativity. Consequently, professorial advisors are likely to adopt a "hands off" or "laissez-faire" attitude toward the student's work. This may leave the student floundering. Guidance is needed for the student to excel in research.

This book addresses the problems of developing and improving research skills and preparing for professional careers. It is a step-by-step guide for students in the life, natural, physical, and social–behavioral sciences. It can also benefit faculty and administrators, and it should be particularly useful to new faculty who wish to organize their thinking on graduate education. The book is designed for self-instruction. It could serve as a text for an introductory "research strategies" course or as an aid for a departmental seminar. It is succinct and can be read quickly, but hints are offered that can be helpful for years. The tips given have been refined through the experiences of noted scientists and educators. The ideas will work if given a try.

I have advised graduate students in a variety of scientific disciplines over the past several years through service as chairman of a university human subjects research committee and as director of an interdisciplinary drug research institute. I have directed or participated in research, and published papers, in the disciplines of analytical chemistry, biochemistry, clinical pharmacy, medicinal chemistry, microbiology, natural products chemistry, organic chemistry, pharmaceutical chemistry, pharmacology, and toxicology. I understand the difficulties graduate students experience in research and in graduate education in general. Problems that stem from a lack of knowledge in course work and in specific research methods, as in statistics or computer programming, are beyond the scope of this book. Rather, impediments regarding approaches, perceptions, and self-initiating efforts are its concerns.

The book is developed in a chronological fashion for the beginning graduate student. The first chapter contains an orientation to graduate research departments. It is followed by chapters on commitments and creativity, making choices (e.g., research problems and an advisor), and managing time. These are followed by chapters on the principles of scientific research and ethics in science. Subsequent chapters are devoted to library research, writing skills, preparing theses and dissertations, and presenting and publishing papers. The book continues with chapters on research with human subjects, animals, and biohazards, and on writing and applying for grants. A concluding chapter provides insights on getting a job in education, government, or industry.

Beginning students can use this book throughout their academic careers. More advanced students may refine skills through its use. In short, this guide should make research a more rewarding and interesting experience.

Many people helped make this book possible. Among my colleagues at the University of Texas at Austin, Professors Betsy E. Bowman (Nursing), Michael J. Churgin (Law), James T. Doluisio (Pharmaceutics), Sheldon Ekland-Olson (Sociology), Carlton Erickson (Pharmacology), Karl A. Folkers (Biomedical Chemistry), Marye Anne Fox (Organic Chemistry), Karl H. Frank (Civil Engineering), Harold D. Grotevant (Home Economics), Marvin L. Hackert (Biochemistry), Laurence H. Hurley (Medicinal Chemistry), T. William Thompson (Petroleum Engineering), David E. Thurston (Medicinal Chemistry), Claire E. Weinstein (Educational Psychology), John A. Wheeler (Physics), and Robert K. Young (Psychology) are singled out for their encouragement and help. I am particularly grateful to Professor Alfred Martin, who reviewed the manuscript and offered wise counsel. Professor Jerry Fineg (Director, Animal Resources Center) supplied most of the references for the animal research section of Chapter 11. Professor Laurence H. Hurley and Professor Jean P. Gagnon (of the University of North Carolina) reviewed several chapters. Professor Gagnon also suggested a number of useful readings. Six chapters were kindly reviewed by Dr. Armand Guarino, Dean of the Graduate School of Biomedical Sciences, University of Texas Health Science Center at San Antonio. A. J. Dusek (Director, Office of Sponsored Projects, University of Texas at Austin) supplied several references and leads to materials on grantsmanship. Aubrey E. Skinner (Librarian, University of Texas at Austin) provided leads to many useful references. Two industrial scientist-administrators have supported my graduate program during the past 10 years: Howard B. Lassman (Hoechst-Roussel Pharmaceuticals Inc.) and Jane C. Sheridan (Hoffmann-La Roche Inc.). Their encouragement and financial help have been essential to my development as a graduate program director. Michael Dews provided editorial assistance, and Marilyn Buchanan contributed persistent and exacting secretarial skills. The editorial staff of ISI Press were of great help with the manuscript. Robert A. Day and Maryanne Soper are singled out for their encouragement and their help with revisions. I am also grateful to the many faculty, postdoctoral fellows, graduate students, and staff who have contributed to research programs in the Drug Dynamics Institute over the past decade. Finally, I acknowledge my wife, Denene Kay Smith, whose moral support helped during this project.

Chapter 1

Getting Started

A strong nor'wester's blowing, Bill,
Hark! Don't ye hear it roar, now?
Lord help 'em, how I pities all
Unhappy folks on shore . . .
                                    —WILLIAM PITT

Entering graduate school marks a turning point in many lives. Graduate education is designed for individual development and growth. With commitment, hard work, and some luck students become independent scholars and researchers. Beginning a graduate career, however, requires knowing who's who and what's what in a graduate research unit and university.

University Organization

Universities are divided into schools and colleges. Thus, a university like the University of Texas at Austin has Colleges of Business Administration, Communication, Education, Engineering, Fine Arts, Liberal Arts, Natural Sciences, and Pharmacy. Additionally, there are Schools of Architecture, Law, Nursing, Public Affairs, and Social Work, along with the Graduate School. Schools and colleges are generally headed by deans who administer a series of departments which in turn are administered by department heads. Certain smaller schools or colleges (i.e., 50 faculty members) may function dually as a collegiate unit and a department. This means that the dean of the smaller school or college also serves as department head. In addition to schools (colleges) and departments, interdisciplinary programs and divisions may be organized through faculty from different academic units.

Interdisciplinary and cross-disciplinary programs offer unusual opportunities for graduate students. Indeed, the student graduating with a

1

combined major may have a competitive career edge over one who is grounded in a single field. One can imagine, for example, unique career opportunities for architecture–civil engineering, biochemistry–pharmacy, and computer science–psychology majors. These kinds of possibilities are important to explore early in a graduate career. An advisor and administrators of a graduate school can help in locating existing opportunities, and in designing personalized programs.

Graduate schools or colleges are uniquely organized. These units have a dean and perhaps a series of associate and assistant deans, but they have no departments. Rather, the graduate school provides an umbrella organization for all graduate programs on campus (see Fig. 1).

The graduate school serves a number of quality-control functions for graduate programs. Through faculty committees and councils, graduate programs are initially reviewed and recommended for approval by the board of governors or regents of the university. Faculty panels and the graduate school dean are also responsible for approval of courses, periodic review of programs, and appointment of graduate faculty. The graduate faculty, in turn, are responsible for day-to-day supervision of graduate students. The heads of departments or specially designated graduate advisors are representatives of the graduate dean in depart-

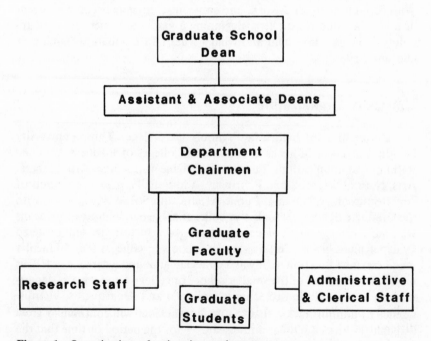

Figure 1 Organization of university graduate programs.

ments, and these representatives are responsible for administering graduate school policies and standards.

The primary mission of graduate research departments is to help develop outstanding scholars and researchers. High-quality departments promote individual freedoms and the vigorous pursuit of knowledge. First-rate departments ring with intellectual excitement—their faculties are anxious to help students execute individual plans of study. This individualized attention sets graduate study apart from baccalaureate and professional programs.

While students are expected to work with advisors in designing customized programs, departmental requirements for core courses, foreign language skills, and candidacy have to be met according to departmental guidelines. Learn these guidelines as soon as possible. If available, obtain the department's guidebook for graduate students. Also, obtain a copy of the graduate school catalog. Make sure that descriptions can be reconciled in both documents. Direct questions to a graduate advisor or other faculty member who may be assigned as a temporary advisor. Be probing with questions. Try to establish quickly how much input students have in each major step of their degree programs.

The Players

Various faculty and staff are encountered during the first few weeks in a graduate research department. The faculty typically consists of professors (also referred to as full professors), associate professors, assistant professors, instructors, and teaching assistants. Professors generally have the greatest seniority and may hold an endowed professorship or chair which is acknowledged by a named title. For example, the noted physicist John A. Wheeler holds the Jane and Roland Blumberg Professorship at the University of Texas at Austin. Endowed positions provide monetary benefits to their holders and are reserved for the most distinguished faculty.

Full professors achieve their rank after vigorous faculty and administrative review which certifies the quality of their scholarship and research. Most noteworthy, promotion from associate professor to professor requires demonstrated competence in directing doctoral-level students. Thus, full professors have a track record for guidance of Ph.D. students.

Associate professors are mid-level academicians who have generally been granted tenure. Tenure is a promissory arrangement. It implies confidence by administration that the faculty member will continue to grow and contribute as a scholar and researcher for the period of time that the faculty person remains at the university. Tenure also guarantees that faculty may pursue their scholarly work without interference from internal or external forces. This is the nature of academic freedom.

Assistant professors are promoted to associate professors after a period of four to seven years. During the trial period, assistant professors must demonstrate research and teaching competencies, and their capabilities to serve the university through faculty committee assignments and other appointments. Accomplishments are evaluated by faculty and administration before tenure is granted. Most importantly, tenure and promotion to associate professor involve an up-or-out decision. If assistant professors are not promoted within a set period (usually six years), they are terminated.

Some graduate research departments have instructor-level faculty. These people may hold Ph.D. degrees, or they may be close to completing their doctoral dissertations.

The teaching faculty is completed with graduate student teaching assistants (TAs). TAs are hired part-time to help faculty with lecture and laboratory courses. TA assignments are made by the department chairman and involve responsibilities to a professorial faculty member who may not be the TA's advisor.

Postdoctoral students or fellows are full-time Ph.D.-level researchers who are supported by grants and contracts. The so-called postdocs report to individual faculty and have few other duties in the department.

Besides postdocs, graduate research departments often have full-time research staff. These people, who may have doctoral degrees, conduct independent research. Thus, they may have a title such as research scientist, research assistant professor, or senior scientist. Research scientist-type individuals are rarely tenured, and they often support themselves through personally obtained grants and contracts. These full-time scientists may consequently be under great pressures. Other full-time research staff include equipment maintenance people, shop workers (e.g., electrical shop, glassblowing shop), and technicians. Technicians are often baccalaureate-level scientists who perform routine research under the supervision of a Ph.D.-level staff or faculty member.

Graduate research departments also have administrative and clerical staff. Purchasing, scheduling, word-processing, and filing are some of the many activities conducted by these essential staff members. Frequently, these staff are overworked, underpaid, and unappreciated. They deserve the respect that should be given to all professionals.

Allegiances and Obligations

Professional development requires allegiances and commitments. Allegiance is owed to science, and to one's university, department, and discipline in that order. Students bear the mark of their university and their discipline—through publication, through résumés, and through contacts with friends and colleagues. After earning a degree, a student's name is tied to his or her department and advisor for life. These associations will be treasured most if good relationships are developed with faculty and colleagues. Faculty-graduate student relationships, in particular, are influenced by students' commitments and independent creative development. These topics are considered in the next chapter.

Chapter 2

Commitments and Creativity

My life is what I have done, my scientific work;
the one is inseparable from the other. The work
is the expression of my inner development. . . .
— C. G. JUNG

Productive and rewarding scholarship and research do not come easily. They require certain personal traits and practices. Some characteristics must already be part of the individual; other personality features, including creativity, can be improved with practice.

Attitudes and Commitments

Research (discovery of new knowledge) and scholarship (organization, criticism, and interpretation of facts and concepts), in and of themselves, can develop commitment. As noted by Katz,[67] many students seem passive and lacking in self-esteem. To become a successful graduate student a take-charge attitude must be adopted — a desire must develop to be creative and productive. These admonitions require commitments that are not fostered by most Americans' habits. For example, excessive television viewing is a deterrent to critical and purposeful observation.

The results of commitment are seen in the lives of successful people in various fields. The tennis player who has just won the Wimbledon Crown, the pianist who has been awarded first place in the International Tchaikovsky Competition, and the recent winner of the Nobel Peace Prize all have something in common. They have committed themselves to a field or a practice for long periods of time. If this is true in sports, as well as in artistic and political areas, then it should not be different for research and scholarship.

Commitment involves an interesting feedback relationship. Reid[106] noted, "It has been my experience that the most unattractive problem be-

6

comes absorbingly interesting when one digs into it . . . when you really get acquainted with a problem, you are apt to fall in love with it." Students who achieve the results necessary to graduate and succeed professionally do so through extraordinary commitment. This commitment, in turn, "fuels" the creativity necessary for greater accomplishments.

A number of practices and occurrences nurture commitment to research and scholarly efforts. Most importantly, highest priority must be given to research and scholarship. Throughout graduate school there are great demands made on students' time. Courses must be taken, seminars attended, and other responsibilities (e.g., teaching assistantships) fulfilled. It is easy to get into the position of "not having enough time for research or scholarship," but research and scholarship are the most important activities in graduate education. Successful students or professionals do not find time for research (scholarship), they *make* time for research (scholarship). This is accomplished by reserving certain times each day and each week for research and scholarly activities. In other words, a day does not go by without some movement toward these goals. At first the necessary discipline may be developed by putting in a minimum amount of time, perhaps only 30 minutes to 1 hour per day. Within weeks or months, it will become difficult to spend so "little" time at research and scholarship—an investment will have been made.

Research and scholarship often involve long-term projects that will require patience to see the project through. This is helped by breaking larger problems into smaller ones and achieving the overall goal in parts. A companion to patience is thoroughness. The proof of a hypothesis must come from experiments that test many different possibilities. This may take much experimentation and data analysis.

Thoroughness is supported by continual summarization and careful documentation of results. A common temptation is to forget negative results and to omit them from research notebooks. This is a serious mistake that can lead to needless repetition of unproductive experimentation.

Conducting research requires a certain level of emotional detachment that allows hypotheses to be challenged and possibly found wrong. This is aided by recording the results of experiments soon after the actual observations, by limiting speculation about results, and by admitting ignorance when appropriate. The last is especially important when engaging in interdisciplinary research in which experiments are performed that involve unfamiliar methods.

Creativity

Creative scientists produce work that is original and is valued by others in the same field. For the beginning graduate student these requirements are difficult because of the implied evaluation of published work which may not appear until after the dissertation is written. There are, however, intervening evaluations of research by advisors and thesis committee members that help the creative development process.

Creative research and scholarship result in a novel product. Newness alone, however, is not enough. For example, an agricultural scientist might find that gold foil provides optimum protection for plants from certain damaging wavelengths of artificially produced sunlight. The obvious cost restriction of this finding limits its usefulness. Thus, for the applied scientist at least, the product must be novel *and* useful—both are criteria used in securing a U.S. patent. In basic research, however, the usefulness of a discovery may not be apparent for years.

In addition to novelty and usefulness, creative research and scholarship involve transformation and condensation. Jackson and Messick[64] defined "transformation" as a property that alters the constraints of reality; a work that defies tradition and yields a new perspective—a work that forces us to *see* reality in a new way. Rocha e Silva[108] noted, "To *see* is to go deep into the meaning of a phenomenon. It is the attitude that leads to the creation of a new theory that may change one's outlook of the universe. . . ." The scientist who *sees* and believes in a new reality is, at the beginning, alone—mistrusted by colleagues and by laymen.[108]

A historically significant example of the transformation characteristic is the discovery of the structural formula for the chemical benzene. For years benzene was know to consist of six atoms of carbon and six atoms of hydrogen (C_6H_6). Many scientists tried to determine how these atoms were arranged to produce the structure of benzene since many combinations and permutations could be conceived. In the late 1800s, Kekulé recorded the event in 1854 that led him to his momentous discovery:

> One fine summer evening, I was returning by the last omnibus, "outside" as usual, through the deserted streets of the metropolis, which are at other times so full of life. I fell into a reverie and lo! the atoms were gambolling before my eyes. . . . I saw how, frequently, two smaller atoms united to form a pair, how a larger one embraced two smaller ones; how still larger ones kept hold of three or even four of the smaller; whilst the whole kept whirling in a giddy dance. I saw how the larger ones formed a chain. . . . I spent part of the night putting on paper at least sketches of these dream forms.[89]

Kekulé benzene, as it later became known, is a resonance hybrid of formulas (Fig. 2) containing an alternating series of single- and double-bonded carbons which account for the C_6H_6 molecular formula and the physicochemical properties of benzene.

Students outside of chemistry may have difficulty appreciating the

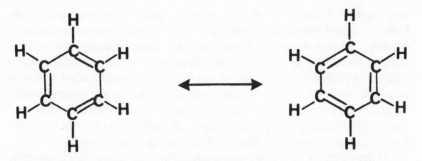

Figure 2   Formulas representing the resonance hybrid of Kekulé benzene.

significance of Kekulé's discovery. Kekulé used what is now referred to as "aha! insight."[53] Through introspection, and the conscious and subconscious "playful" manipulation of ideas, a novel mixture of concepts resulted which became the structural representation for benzene. Aha! insight is probably enhanced by playing mathematical and computer-based games, and by taking advantage of certain subconscious influences which are discussed in Chapter 5

The final necessary characteristic of creative research and scholarship is condensation. This is exemplified by works that encompass many ideas. Jackson and Messick[64] noted that these works are, "Products [discoveries] that warrant close and repeated examination [and] . . . do not divulge their total meaning on first viewing. These products offer something new each time we experience them. . . . They have about them an intensity and concentration of meaning requiring continued contemplation." Darwin's theory of evolution represents a work that rates high in condensation because it has helped explain the origins of animal life from discoveries made through a variety of research efforts during the last century.

People are frequently misled by the term "theory" as it is used in science and as it applies to a theory like evolution. The debate on teaching creationism versus evolution in schools, for example, often focuses on the notion that evolution is just a theory which is not proved. Yet, scientific theories are never fully proved. Rather, they become more and more accepted as proofs develop. Eventually, theories are replaced by broader theories, and the process of proofs continues.

Levels of Creativity

The word "creativity" is used loosely in society. It tends to be confused with popularity, productivity, and professional visibility. Also, people may be called creative when they achieve modest goals such as winning first place in a high school essay contest or science fair. These individuals are better described as amateur creatives. Advanced-level creative scientists or *auctors* (from the Latin meaning maker, builder, author, or inventor), as noted by Mansfield and Busse,[83] produce works that embody novelty, value, transformation, and condensation. It might be asked, however, what traits and practices lead to auctor-level work? Simultaneously it should be acknowledged that there are no quantum leaps within the realm of auctors. Rather, a continuum of creativity exists from amateur creatives to advanced researchers and scholars.

There appear to be three preconditions for auctor-level scientific creativity: above average intelligence, extensive training in the field, and emotional balance. For graduate students, the first prerequisite is met through entrance requirements (i.e., grades and GRE scores) of graduate programs. The need for extensive training is evident, and the importance of commitment has been previously emphasized. Also, the specialization and depth of study required of graduate students takes time. Students should not feel discouraged if they seem initially to lack creative insights. Often, creative insights barely start to develop during the last year or so of a graduate career. Some scientists feel that creativity only starts to blossom after several years of research.

Roe[109] proposed that a minimal level of emotional adjustment is necessary for creative research and scholarship. Indeed, only the emotionally stable individual will be able to develop the persistence and commitment that are needed for in-depth study. Some researchers believe that persistence and commitment are related to the pleasure derived from being alone and from one's level of self-confidence. Many students have the prerequisites for becoming an auctor-level creative scientist. To develop perspective, however, the traits of acknowledged creative scientists are reviewed below.

Characteristics of Auctors

MacKinnon[79] described six characteristics that are associated with creative scientists:

1. Autonomy
2. Personal flexibility and openness
3. Need for originality
4. Need for recognition
5. Commitment to work
6. Aesthetic sensitivities

Auctors are autonomous. They display independence and accept nothing on blind faith, or on the mere say-so of "authorities." Autonomy should be promoted in graduate programs, and it will be nurtured by good advisors. Indeed, a criterion for choosing an advisor is the advisor's reputation for fostering graduate student autonomy.

Creative scientists are flexible and open to new experience and interpretations. They are unconcerned with strict adherence to rules and regulations, and they reject dogmatic behavior. While a lack of dogmatism is critical, the researcher must adhere to some prescribed routines as they occur in experimental protocols (strict sets of directions for experiments as used most often in human subjects research). Also, successful creative scientists adopt a sense of professionalism in meeting deadlines and in dealings with support staff. These characteristics involve habits that should be reinforced during graduate school. Flexibility and openness require the toleration of uncertainty and complexity. Creative scientists have faith that good experimental design and persistence will lead to truth through research.

It requires courage to attempt new experimental routines and procedures. For the beginning graduate student, the fear of new methods or techniques can hamper progress in research. This is counteracted, in part, by choosing an advisor who helps overcome these apprehensions. For example, the establishment of a hierarchical structure in research groups provides role models for new graduate students and provides mechanisms for helping all students progress. A good advisor also helps students learn the difference between ideas and good ideas. This is indicated in part by the quality of the journals that have published work of the advisor's former students.

Auctors need to be original and novel. They consciously strive to achieve those goals which relate to the importance of ego and high levels of self-esteem. The need for originality, however, transcends science. It is observed in creative members of other fields. For example, Thorton Wilder, the Pulitzer Prize winning author of "Our Town," once noted, [138] "I erase as I go along . . . I look forward so much I have only an imperfect memory for the past. When your eyes are directed to the future, you have no hurt feelings over the praises or criticism of the moment—because, moment by moment, the present becomes the past. You have the sense of forever beginning your career, of trying to offer something new to interest the community."

Wilder's conviction expresses a need for professional recognition that is also a prominent trait among creative researchers and scholars. This trait is exemplified by disputes scientists have had over priority claims to research findings. In this connection, auctors are more likely to be assertive than humble, and they jealously guard their lifestyles.

From earlier discussion it may not be surprising to learn that auctors show high levels of commitment. Mansfield and Busse[83] described several studies showing that creative scientists work longer and harder, and are more productive, than their less creative peers. Retrospective studies also suggest that the commitment begins in graduate school.

It has been noted by MacKinnon[79] and Zuckerman[141] that auctorive-level researchers experience aesthetic satisfaction from their work. Creative researchers find beauty in science and in solutions to problems. Their commitment is fostered by gratification experienced after proving hypotheses through personally designed and conducted (or directed) experimentation.

In summary, auctor-level scientists need to be original and seek professional recognition. They are committed to their work, and they display flexibility and openness to experience; they act autonomously and find beauty in their work. This montage serves as a model and as the basis of a plan for self-determined improvement.

The plan will be influenced by conscious choices and to some degree by chance. Four types of chance have been described by Austin.[6] Blind luck (Chance I) is independent of personal characteristics and functions equally in everyone's life. Chance II or good luck results from general exploratory behavior. The more one reads, experiments, and practices introspection, the greater the chance that random ideas will occur in certain juxtaposition to spark creative discovery.

Chance III is associated with serendipity and with Pasteur's assertion that chance favors the prepared mind. This type of luck occurs with experience and requires a degree of courage to face the initially inexplicable result. Experienced investigators know that research frequently involves pursuit of unusual data points. Many important discoveries were, initially, findings that were discordant with expected results. The "unprepared mind" has the tendency to discard such results and begin again, thinking that the experiment went wrong. The more experienced researcher, however, will meet the serendipitous challenge by performing additional experimentation and by modifying hypotheses as necessary.

Chance IV provides fortuitous ideas through individualized action. Businessmen choose sports activities such as golf because of the advantageous contacts that are made during play. Hobbies or leisure time activities can be chosen to complement scientific work. For example, graduate students in mechanical engineering could reinforce their research pursuits by having an interest in auto repair. Marine biology students might take up scuba diving. This can be referred to as "making things count double."

The development of auctor-level scientists is dependent on choices made throughout graduate school. Some of these choices will be required during the first few months of graduate school and are considered in the next chapter.

Chapter 3

Making Choices

*All I have learnt of any value
has been self-taught.*
— CHARLES DARWIN

Plans for becoming a creative researcher and scholar involve choices. The type of research chosen, the choice of research advisor or other role models and support, the selection of a research problem and the proper tools to solve it, and the choice of thesis or dissertation committee members all involve thoughtful decisions.

Types of Research

Research is often subdivided into two types — basic and applied. Basic research involves study of the fundamental properties of subjects and their behavior. Applied research focuses on the usefulness of subjects and their behavior. "Subjects" is used broadly to include materials, animals, and human beings. Stated differently, basic research enables us to seek truth; applied research tends to serve our material well-being.

Basic research is sometimes maligned because of the perceived unimportance of specific projects. Senator Proxmire's so-called Golden-Fleece awards[104] have been issued periodically for government-sponsored projects thought to be silly or useless. Some of these awards have gone to basic biomedical and social–behavioral research efforts. Yet, the apparently useless basic research of today may serve as a necessary precursor to vital applied work of tomorrow. The key factor is the quality of the research rather than the specific projects or objectives. Both basic and applied research are essential, and the choice of one or the other should not be influenced by prejudices. The choice of basic or applied research should also be based on personal needs.

Basic research requires an extraordinary dedication to narrow purposes. This is compatible with individuals who enjoy isolation and who relish the idea of becoming world experts in a limited area. Basic researchers work at the frontier. Equipment and other experimental tools necessary to solve problems may not be commercially available. In the physical sciences, for example, equipment will usually have to be constructed. This requires an aptitude for mechanical, electronic, and computer-science skills. Applied researchers, on the other hand, will generally be able to use currently available electronic and computer-based equipment, perhaps with minor modifications.

An applied researcher engages in projects that are thought to offer immediate benefit to society. Consequently, this type of research may fulfill an inner need to help people. During their careers, applied researchers are likely to interact with greater numbers of people than their colleagues engaged in basic research. Also, applied researchers may have greater opportunities for funding of research proposals, for professional consulting, and for the development of combination career goals such as: teacher/scientist, manager/scientist, or counselor/scientist.

Applied research is more likely to provide quick results than its basic counterpart. The psychic rewards of basic research, however, may be greater than those of applied research. The choice of basic or applied research should therefore be made according to personal and professional preferences.

Choosing an Advisor

Advisors have powerful influences on graduate students' research. Thus, it is important to assess the advantages of different types of advisors and to find an advisor who supports creativity and who interacts well with students. There are generally three types of advisors: (1) the collaborator type, (2) the hands-off type, and (3) the senior scientist type.

Collaborator types are likely to be young academically (i.e., assistant professors), and they are keen to have their students achieve quick results. These advisors generally have more time for research because of light administrative duties. In the laboratory-based fields, this means that collaborators work side-by-side with students at the bench. In social–behavioral areas the collaborator may assist with data collection and analysis. Collaborator advisors have a vested interest in their students' research results. In some disciplines this means joint publications. In other fields, the collaborator advisor merely receives credit for advising students who complete degree requirements. Regardless of the field, publications and graduate students are of vital importance to this advisor, who may be seeking promotion and tenure. Because of a need for productivity, the collaborator advisor may bias choices of research problems. The need for results may cause this advisor to encourage students to tackle problems of low risk and low significance.

The hands-off advisor is generally at mid-level academically and is likely to have administrative responsibilities. These advisors have less time to spend on projects directly, but they may be less "greedy" for results. This is a two-sided issue. This advisor may allow excessive time to complete work. Hands-off advisors may be sources of wise counsel, and they will encourage pursuit of problems of comparatively higher risk and significance.

Senior scientist advisors are well-established faculty. These advisors have varying amounts of time to commit to students. The quality of attention, however, may be the best of all because of their extensive past experience. If a senior advisor is an outstanding researcher in her or his field, a master scientist–student relationship may ensue. This has been shown to be of substantial benefit. Indeed, Mansfield and Busse[83] pointed out that more than half of American Nobel Prize winners worked under Nobel Laureates of earlier generations. In some instances, however, senior scientist advisors are living on past glories and may have become obsolete in their fields. Working with these individuals can lead to minor research problems and to the unfortunate possibility of being trained in outdated methods.

All types of advisors will display various professional and personal characteristics. Of prime importance is the advisor's reputation as a scientist. This can be judged by his or her *curriculum vitae*, which can be obtained either before or during a personal interview. Determine how many papers the prospective advisor has published in high-quality journals. Select a number of the apparently important citations and check them through *Science Citation Index*. This provides an indication of how often the advisor's work is cited by others, and that is a measure of its importance.

Determine how many invited presentations and consultantships the prospective advisor has had during the past five years. Check to see how many grants this advisor has successfully competed for during her or his career. Make inquiries about the reputation of the prospective advisor as a teacher. It is also important to see how many students have graduated under this advisor's direction. Try to determine the current position and rank of former students. All of these factors are measures of the stature of the prospective advisor.

In a field involving laboratory research, ask to see prospective advisors' laboratories in operation. Visit with graduate students working in these laboratories. Note the number of professionals managed by the advisors. A research group of more than 10 individuals, including graduate students, postdoctoral fellows, and technicians, is unwieldy except for the most talented academic managers.

Ask about the organizational structure of the laboratory. Are there hierarchical systems for helping graduate students who are new members of the group? For example, many advisors have a big brother system in which novices are assigned to a senior graduate student or postdoctoral fellow for several months to a year for day-to-day training. Other systems may have been developed to help newcomers achieve sufficient training to permit independent experimentation. Find out if these systems have existed for some time and if they seem to function well. Make sure the advisor has grant funds to cover research costs. This is of vital importance since few departments have sufficient intramural funds to support outstanding laboratory research.

Choose an advisor who is demanding. The best advisors are those who require periodic reports, meet regularly with students either individually or collectively, and expect a high level of performance.

An advisor should have a personality and management style that favor creative development. Good advisors promote the traits of auctors that were discussed in Chapter 2. Of particular importance are the following: (1) respect for individuality, (2) enthusiasm and personal support, (3) patience, and (4) recognition. Does the prospective advisor respect student contributions? Does the advisor have a record of encouraging students to contribute ideas and judgments in joint research efforts? How enthusiastic is the prospective advisor about previous students' achievements? Does the prospective advisor have a history of patience with students and their developmental problems? One measure of this is prior success in directing students as indicated in part by student turnover. Have students who studied under this advisor graduated regularly and in a timely fashion during the past five years? Does the advisor have a record of losing students?

What kind of recognition has the prospective advisor given to students in the past? Has she or he arranged for students to present papers at scientific meetings? In joint research in which the student's efforts were paramount, does the student's name appear first on resultant publications?

During a personal interview with the prospective advisor, engage in conversation that will answer the questions raised in the above paragraphs. If the advisor seems vague or evasive on points raised, he or she may have deficiencies. After talking, ask to visit with some of his or her current students. The resulting discussions must be done tactfully and with the caution that needs to be applied to hearsay information.

One method for choosing an advisor is to work with a potential advisor on a trial basis for a semester. This is the best way to evaluate the advisor's management style and compatibility. The trial procedure may be mandated by departmental policy. In some departments students are expected to rotate among two or three faculty before choosing an advisor. Having a university fellowship or teaching assistantship may provide the advantage of being in the department for one to six months before having to choose an advisor. This situation provides the necessary time for an evaluation.

In summary, the choice of an advisor should be based on the prospective advisor's:

- accomplishments in teaching and research
- enthusiasm for advising students
- experience in directing graduate students
- management and organization of his or her research group
- reputation for demanding excellence
- compatible personality

Despite all efforts, an incompatible advisor may be chosen. Problems can sometimes be worked out through honest communication. If not, it is important to change advisors despite fears of being branded. Actually, changes in students' preferences have happened to most advisors, and they are not as shocked by changes as some students might imagine.

Role Models

It is useful to adopt role models. These should consist of departmental faculty and graduate students, and other researchers. The faculty and researcher role models should have talents complementary to those of an advisor. Graduate student role models should be representative of the different stages of one's graduate career (e.g., first-year students and students already admitted to candidacy).

Financial Support

Graduate students are supported in one of three ways: (1) teaching assistantship, (2) research assistantship, or (3) research fellowship. Most teaching assistantships are half-time appointments that include a 20-hour commitment per week to teaching in the department. The teaching responsibilities may range from grading papers to teaching one or more courses. Before accepting a teaching assistantship find out what specific duties are required. Some departments are not as stringent as others with time commitments. A strict 20 hours per week may not be expected though this can vary during different portions of a semester.

Research assistantships, like teaching assistantships, typically involve half-time appointments. Research assistantships are developed through grant funds and require commitment to a specific project. The grant holder or principal investigator may or may not be an advisor. By working for an advisor, it may be possible to dovetail the responsibilities of the research assistantship with the objectives of thesis research. Alternatively, research may be performed that is unrelated to dissertation research. Choosing a research assistantship is like selecting an advisor. In addition, the nature of the project is important along with its compatibility with research goals.

Research fellowships involve support with no expectation that specific tasks will be performed. This type of support is ideal because it permits complete devotion to thesis research and course work. The level of support is usually similar to that available through assistantships.

The research assistantship or fellowship that supports work necessary to earn a degree may be tax exempt. Regulations enumerated under Internal Revenue Service (IRS) ruling 60-378,[126] or its equivalent, and the judgment of departmental administration should be consulted before making this determination.

Programs of Study

Many departments develop rigid policy on programs of study for graduate degrees. Other units may have looser approaches to graduate education. Ideally, a program of study should be flexible yet provide core knowledge needed for performance as a researcher.

If the modal Ph.D. degree requires four years of study, two plans for completion of course work and research can be proposed as indicated in Figure 3. Plan A stresses research throughout the graduate career whereas Plan B provides for exclusive block-efforts, first in course work and then in research. Adoption of plan A requires early research activities that may not be possible in all fields. This type of plan, however, emphasizes the importance of research in graduate training which was proposed earlier. Also, plan A, with its integration of course work and research, requires careful time management. Development of this skill in graduate school will be beneficial in a subsequent career.

A disadvantage of plan A is that course work necessary to pursue certain aspects of research may not be completed in a timely fashion. This is the major advantage of plan B and is the reason many departments adopt this approach through core curricula or equivalent mechanisms.

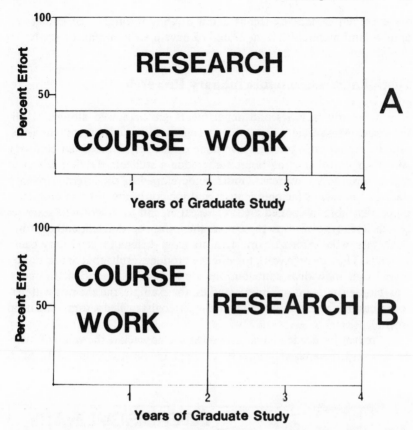

Figure 3 Diagrammatic representations of models for doctoral study. Approximate formal course equivalents: A, 25 to 30 semester hours (= 40% of years 0 to 3.3); B, 40 to 50 semester hours (50% of years 0 to 4). (Reprinted with permission from R. V. Smith, Doctoral education for the pharmaceutical industry, Drug Devel. Ind. Pharm. **7**:461–482, 1981. Copyright by Marcel Dekker Inc.)

Plan B is often attractive to graduate students because it appears less risky. It can be comforting to think, "When I have developed all the tools necessary to do my research work, then I will start." This is naive because research stimulates and reinforces learning. Indeed, material learned from experimental work will be retained better and with greater understanding than that gained through course work.

Plans A and B involve compromises. Some permutation of these plans should be developed to meet the demands of the discipline and an advisor. For example, some graduate courses involve mini-research projects. Other courses may have requirements such as the preparation of research proposals which will lead to ideas for dissertation projects. These are examples of making things count double. Regardless of choices of courses and research, it is desirable to have a written plan of study.

Disciplinary vs. Interdisciplinary Research

University faculties and departments are organized along disciplinary lines. Most faculty are devoted to research that advances their fields, and, by definition, work in a discipline is narrowly focused. Disciplinary work is a useful starting point for graduate students. During advancement, however, an awareness must be developed of the interdisciplinary nature of problems facing scientists and society. Many of these problems, especially those in applied areas of research, call for interdisciplinary research. This type of research involves the joint, coordinated, and continuously integrated efforts of investigators from different disciplinary backgrounds. These people work together to produce results that are so tightly woven that individual contributions are not easily identified. In chemical–biological interdisciplinary studies, for example, the chemist will perform biological experiments, and the biologist will do some chemical work.

Progressive academicians and scientists appreciate the value of interdisciplinary research efforts. The eminent biochemist Esmond E. Snell noted[118]:

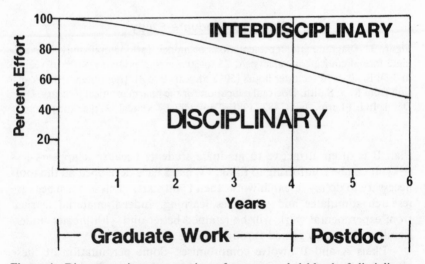

Figure 4 Diagrammatic representation of recommended blend of disciplinary and interdisciplinary work in doctoral and postdoctoral studies. (Reprinted with permission from R. V. Smith. Doctoral education for the pharmaceutical industry, Drug Devel. Ind. Pharm. 7:461–482, 1981. Copyright by Marcel Dekker Inc.)

. . . knowledge, unlike universities, cannot be segmented along departmental lines. . . . progress at the frontier of knowledge is most rapid when a variety of investigational techniques is applied . . . Departmental structures, while useful and necessary for administrative and instructional purposes, reflect the historical development of a subject area and cannot anticipate future needs in it. If too rigidly or jealously maintained, they can inhibit the very development they seek to promote.

Snell's position should not be misconstrued. Interdisciplinary research is no substitute for good disciplinary training during the greater part of a graduate career. It is advisable, however, to seek exposure to interdisciplinary activities in graduate as well as postdoctoral training (see Fig. 4) since most researchers engage in interdisciplinary research during their professional careers.

Research Problem

Following are points to consider when choosing a research problem:

1. Can it be enthusiastically pursued?
2. Can interest be sustained by it?
3. Is the problem solvable?
4. Is it worth doing?
5. Will it lead to other research problems?
6. Is it manageable in size?
7. What is its potential for making original contributions to the literature?
8. If the problem is solved, will it be reviewed well by scholars in your field?
9. Are you, or will you become, competent to solve it?
10. By solving it, will you have demonstrated independent skills in your discipline?
11. Will the necessary research prepare you in an area of demand or promise for the future in your field?

The choice of a research problem should be a highly personalized decision. It may involve background, interests, perceived research strengths, aesthetic judgments, and personal commitments. Some students in the biomedical sciences choose research related to a disease state that afflicted a relative or close friend. Students in social–behavioral sciences may feel deeply about a particular social injustice or condition. These "biases" can actually become the foundation for commitments that will last for years, or a lifetime.

Another important basis for the choice of a research problem can be the professional opportunities it leads to after graduation. Miller and Shay,[88] chief executive officers of the Stanford Research Institute, have forecasted that the scientific areas of greatest commercial exploitation through the year 2000 will be:

- Information technology — microelectronics, microprocessor chips, and fiber optics
- New materials and their applications — composite polymers, ceramic turbine engines, and synthetic membranes
- Factory and office automation — artificial vision and machine sensing of touch, force, and torque, robotics, and machine-human interactions
- Biotechnology — genetic engineering and recombinant DNA technology, production of industrial chemicals and microelectronic memory, production of pharmaceutical products including protein hormones and vaccines
- Health and medical technology — new drug delivery systems, tissue culture methods for the study of disease and toxicological testing of drugs and industrial chemicals, ultrasonic-computer and positron-emission tomography, organic electronic systems for diagnosis and treatment of illnesses, drug design through molecular engineering, drugs to alter brain function and consciousness, and irradiation processes

These industrial developments will require analytical chemists, biochemists, biomedical engineers, chemical engineers, computer scientists, electrical engineers, mechanical engineers, medicinal chemists, microbiologists, molecular biologists, neuropharmacologists, pharmaceutical scientists, physicists, physiologists, physical chemists, polymer chemists, psychologists, radiation biologists, and toxicologists with state-of-the-art training. Are these opportunities of interest?

The choice of a research problem may be dictated in part by an already-funded research project. In such a case, objectives have to be meshed with those in the grant proposal. Some lack of enthusiasm in the project at first may be replaced by intensified interest when the project evolves, as indicated earlier.

As noted by Medawar,[84] solvable problems are those involving hypotheses that can be tested by practicable experiments. Worthy research problems are also fundable and lead to many other problems. Indeed, one of the most commonly asked questions at dissertation orals is something like, "If you could remain a few more years, what problems would you pursue as uncovered by your dissertation research?" Such a question contains an element of irony for the candidate who typically cannot conceive of spending any more time on campus. Yet, this candidate may extend the doctoral research, especially if he or she goes on to an academic career. Some academicians have misgivings about this prospect. Nevertheless, the choice of a research problem that is fundable can be of immense benefit later.

A research problem must be solvable in a reasonable time period and must have potential for contributions to the literature. Madsen[80] suggested that the latter objective is met if the problem does one or more of the following:

- Uncovers new facts
- Suggests new relationships
- Challenges currently accepted truths or assumptions
- Provides new insights into poorly understood phenomena

By meeting one or more of these objectives, the resulting work should be regarded highly by others, including members of a dissertation committee. By solving a challenging and significant problem, skills will have been demonstrated that should certify competence in a discipline.

Courses and Research Aids

Courses are chosen on the basis of core curricula requirements or disciplinary objectives in the plan of study. Courses that provide tools of research should also be considered (e.g., computer science, statistics, technical writing).

Various professional societies and commercial publishers have developed film, software, tape, and slide-tape materials that are useful adjuncts to formally organized course work. For example, the American Chemical Society[5] has audio courses with diverse titles such as: "Probability and Statistics for Chemists," "Effective Utilization of Time," "Applied Problem Solving Through Creative Thinking," "Practical Technical Writing," and "Use of the Chemical Literature." The Media Review Digest (MRD)[85] describes all types of media. This guide also includes overall quality ratings based on editorial reviews. For example, the following entry appears in the 1979 MRD:

Hypothesis Testing
(Series: Inferential Statistics)
John Wiley Films; The Media guide, 1977.
16 mm   25 min   sd   col $365.00   r:$35.00
This program considers random assignments of subjects to groups, the formation of a statistical hypothesis, errors of decision, and other topics relevant to hypothesis testing.
(Science — General)   1) Statistics 001.422

Gr 12–C + Previews v7 n4, Dec, 1978.
p 15. St. George, A.

Acquisition ($365.00) and rental costs ($35.00) are provided along with recommended audience levels (Gr 12–C) and citations of published reviews (Previews etc.). Other guides to audiovisual materials and software are available,[42,43] including a listing of materials[43] that can be ordered by your university library free of charge.

Competency in foreign languages used to be a common requirement of doctoral programs. Many universities now permit substitution of tools of research (e.g., statistics, computer science) for language requirements. Yet, knowledge of foreign languages may be important to students' career goals. Social–behavioral scientists such as sociologists and social psychologists should consider developing a reading and speaking knowledge of Spanish because of the rapidly growing Hispanic communities in many parts of the country. History of science scholars should plan studies of German and French.

In general, the use of languages other than English has diminished in importance in science in recent years. Most journals publish articles in English, and international meetings rarely exclude presentations in English. Knowledge of foreign languages, however, facilitates international collaborative efforts that are common among scientists. All of the above factors should be weighed when deciding on foreign language study.

Thesis and Dissertation Committee Members

Masters' theses and doctoral dissertations are supervised by committees consisting of the following numbers of faculty members: M.S., three to four; Ph.D., four to six. An advisor chairs the committee, which is usually chosen one to three years before a degree is awarded.

Students often have input in the selection of their committee members. Thus, it is useful to begin early to note potential candidates. Faculty who are young academically are often most helpful during thesis and dissertation work because of their lighter commitments. These faculty may also be the most demanding. The guidelines suggested for choosing an advisor are also valuable in selecting dissertation or thesis committee members.

Sometimes research problems involve a significant component from an allied field. A physical chemistry graduate student, for example, may have to construct an electronic apparatus to test and collect data on molten metal mixtures. A faculty member from electrical engineering would be a valuable asset as a member of the student's committee. In an analogous situation, a genetics student may require complex statistical designs for studies of mutations in *Drosophila* species. This student would be well advised to seek out a member of the statistics faculty for service on her or his committee.

Graduate work involves numerous choices. Many of these have been discussed above. One of the most important choices, however, involves the use of time, which is considered in the next chapter

Chapter 4

Time Management

Dost thou love life? Then do not squander time;
for that's the stuff life is made of.
— BENJAMIN FRANKLIN

Time is asymmetric. It moves inexorably forward — it waits for no person. Effective use of time requires planning, and methods for organizing and executing plans.

Planning

Everyone has goals. Many people, however, do not reach their goals for lack of planning. Three sets of goals should be developed: lifetime, intermediate, and short term.[72]

Lifetime goals should be written out. These goals should be lucid and measurable. For example, the goal to win a major research prize is clear and measurable. In contrast, a goal to appreciate research in an allied field is fuzzy or unmeasurable. Other lifetime goals might include publishing a certain number of refereed books or articles, earning a departmental chairmanship at a major state university, successfully competing for a grant from the National Science Foundation, and securing a consultantship with a Fortune 500 corporation. A list of lifetime goals should be reviewed periodically.

Intermediate goals relate to outcomes during the next few years. For the beginning doctoral student, intermediate goals may include completion of course work, preparation of a doctoral research proposal, and achieving candidacy. Like lifetime goals, these are measurable and clearly stated.

Short-term goals involve outcomes expected during the next 12 months. These goals are more performance oriented, and they help with achievement of intermediate goals. Examples of short-term goals are

26

earning an A in a course, learning how to program a computer, and performing an experiment.

A list of intermediate and short-term goals becomes a To Do List. Items on one's To Do List should be classified by priority — for example, with the letters A, B, and C.[72] Following are characteristics of these priorities.

Priority A
1. Critical
2. May be unpleasant to do
3. Goal related
4. Must be done today

Priority B
1. Important
2. Goal related
3. Must be done soon, but not today

Priority C
1. Can wait
2. May or may not be goal related
3. No significant time pressure
4. Usually easy, quick, and pleasant

After scanning this list, you may have properly concluded that A's are the most difficult, but highest priority, items. Similarly, Lakein[72] stated that 80 percent of one's goals are achieved by completing 20 percent of the most important items on a To Do List — the A's.

Despite the importance of A-priority items, there are many temptations to work on C's. The latter are easy to accomplish, take little time, and involve the pleasure of completing something that can be crossed off the To Do List. Ways should be found to resist this temptation. B-priority items are important and become A's with time. Planning itself is never less than a B-priority item.

A transition from B to A can be represented by a paper that may be due in a core course taken during a fall term. A December 15 deadline may be known during the first week of September. The paper may be a B-priority item on the To Do List in September and October. As November approaches the paper becomes an A-priority item. The timing for this type of transition has to be customized. Dealing with A and B items in this way, however, creates reminders of impending deadlines. It also forces planning.

C-priority items rarely become A's and can often be avoided. One way of doing this is to have a drawer or box where C-related materials are tossed.[72] On occasion these C items might be reviewed and many dumped. Examples of C activities are reading brochures for books and taking elective courses. C activities are often "nice to do" but they are not necessary to achieve important goals.

Continually pursuing A items can be helped by using a Daily To Do List prepared at the end of each previous working day. This separate To Do List may be on a small lined pad that is broken into two sections: Things To Do and Follow-up. The pad is dated at the top and A items are listed in priority order: A-1, A-2, A-3, etc. These A-priority items might include turning in a report that is due, completing a necessary experiment, and attending a scheduled meeting with an advisor. Follow-up items are holdovers from the previous day. Each day, an attempt should be made to accomplish everything on the Daily To Do List.

Like a Daily To Do List, all papers handled should be dated. The dated materials become additional subtle reminders of work left undone or of impending deadlines.

Organization

The development of goals and the use of To Do Lists are essential for the organization of research and scholarly work. Of equal importance is the daily routine. There are times during the day when we are most alert and creative. For some, this may be from seven to nine in the morning; others work best during evening hours. The "prime time" should be reserved for tasks that require greatest ingenuity. "Down periods" can be reserved for less mentally demanding tasks such as running a routine experiment or transcribing notes. Once an effective schedule has been found, it should be maintained.

Unusual schedules should be considered carefully. Some students say that they work best at night. This type of student may occasionally work throughout the night, but is often missing from the department during daytime hours. Unusual efforts such as these are acceptable for extraordinary students, but for the average or slightly above average student, typical daytime routines are preferable.

It is useful to organize work space areas and to learn how to properly order supplies and chemicals. Most universities have involved rules for purchasing. A copy of the rules can be posted in the work area for future reference. It is also important to learn how purchase order numbers function so that checks can be made on orders that are delayed or canceled by vendors. Copies of all purchase orders should be kept in a separate file for reference.

The time spent organizing research areas and learning rules may seem wasted, but this time will save many hours over a period of years. It is also important to determine what kind of help is available for scholarly and research work. In laboratory-based sciences, maintenance shops should be located that can be used for repair and construction of equipment. An advisor should be questioned about budgetary constraints that may limit the use of these services.

Many professors hire work-study students to perform routine clerical and laboratory tasks. Work-study students are undergraduates who are paid a nominal hourly wage for 10 to 20 hours of work per week. The federal government provides 80 percent of their salary, and the balance is generated through grants or departmental funds. Funds may be available to hire a work-study student to do routine laboratory or literature work. This can save considerable time.

All researchers have to engage in routine tasks, but the time spent on these tasks can be used more effectively by simultaneously thinking about previous experiments and planning new experiments. For example, the neurobiologist setting up an electrophysiological experiment may mentally review the fundamentals of nerve function. A geologist collecting rock specimens in the field could give thought to crystal habits of commonly occurring minerals. The investigator on an archeological dig might mentally survey the historical antecedents of the excavation site. This habit has been used by many researchers and is possibly a source of allusions to the "absent-minded scholar." For example, Nathaniel Hawthorne developed ideas for four of his novels, including *The Scarlet Letter*, while performing routine duties in the Customs House in Salem, Massachusetts.[72] Einstein devised many of his most important concepts on relativity and quantum theory while working as a clerk in the Patent Office in Berne, Switzerland.[95]

The effective use of work periods should relieve guilt about leisure time. In fact, time for personal interests and for relaxation can further professional interests. It was noted earlier that hobbies can lead to reading and activities that benefit creativity. Nalimov[91] suggested that moments during the most trivial activities can provide useful insights from the subconscious or sudden spiked entries into the continuous consciousness. Thus, pen and notepad should be available at all times to capture "brilliant" thoughts.

Execution

With goals set and routines organized, timely execution should be sought. The first step in executing tasks effectively is to identify time wasters. MacKenzie[78] listed the most common ones as follows:

1. Telephone interruptions
2. Ineffective use of the telephone

3. Visitors dropping in without notice
4. Crisis situations
5. Lack of deadlines
6. Not sticking to high-priority work
7. Indecision and procrastination
8. Over-involvement with detail and routine
9. Attempting too much
10. Underestimating the time to perform tasks
11. Poor communication
12. Inability to say "no"
13. Boredom, fatigue, and ill health

These time wasters can have significant impact over a year, and ways should be found to minimize their influence. Of particular importance are interruptions, such as visitors dropping by unannounced. These encounters occasionally lead to beneficial exchanges of ideas. Indeed, Pelz and Andrews noted[98] that generous interactions between scientists improve their effectiveness. Idle contacts or chit-chat sessions, however, are major time wasters. Friends who drop by every other morning to report their latest feats in racquetball are performing a disservice. In discouraging intrusions of this type, body language is a useful aid. The intruder who is met at the door or greeted by your standing up is less likely to sit, relax, and proceed to waste 30 minutes of precious time. Similarly, overdrawn dialogue is quickly brought to completion by your standing up and walking with the person out of the room. Other assertiveness measures such as honestly noting a need to get back to work must be used with slower characters.

Deadlines improve performance. They provide some stress, or dither, that enhances creativity. Weaver[132] adopted an unusual meaning for the word "dither." He recounted how British engineers during World War II built a constant state of minor but rapid vibration into antiaircraft weaponry. It was thought that, if the guns were constantly in slight motion, this would free them from static friction and make them more responsive. For scientists, "dither" is a frequent state of mental excitement which is perpetuated by deadlines and friendly jostling of ideas by colleagues. The mental excitement is largely self-imposed but is bolstered by deadlines set by outside agencies (e.g., deadlines for submission of grant proposals).

Speed reading is often suggested as a means to save time. The scientist, however, must read carefully and slowly to weigh hypotheses and evaluate results and conclusions. While reading, questions should be asked such as: Was the experimental work well planned? Were the experiments carried out well? Are the conclusions supported by the data? What additional experimentation might be called for to fully support the hy-

© 1961 United Feature Syndicate, Inc.

pothesis? In coping with the tremendous increases in literature, priority consciousness in choosing reading material is more important than concern with reading faster.

Poor communications can result in serious time losses. Following are activities that can improve communications:

- Arrange regularly scheduled meetings with an advisor.
- Organize appointments.
- Take notes and use verbal feedback (e.g., "If I understand correctly, you're saying that . . .") during research meetings.

The remaining hindrances to effective time management are boredom, fatigue, and illness. Boredom is reduced by diversity. Blending experimentation with writing and studying is helpful. This type of diversity has been shown to benefit productivity and creativity of scientists. All work can be broken up by occasional personal rewards.

In summary, fulfilling plans for graduate and professional careers will require careful organization and execution. These are accomplished through the use of To Do Lists and a conscious attempt to minimize time wasters. Efforts to improve time management will be of great help in completing experimental work, the principles of which are covered in the next chapter.

Chapter 5

Principles of Scientific Research

*Our amazing industrial development has been made
possible by the vast accumulation of scientific
knowledge and technical know-how, every single
item of which is a result of someone's observing,
thinking, and experimenting, that is, of research.*
—EBENEZER E. REID

Scientific research has provided knowledge and understanding that
has freed man from the ignorance that once promoted fear, mysticism,
superstition, and illness. Developments in science and scientific methods,
however, did not occur easily. Many of our ancestors had to face religious
and political persecution, even death, because they dared to advance the
notion that knowledge and understanding could be gained through systematic study and practice. Today, the benefits of scientific research are
understood. We appreciate the advances in the biological and physical
sciences that allow the control of environment, the probing of the universe, and communications around the globe. We also appreciate the advances in biochemistry and molecular biology that have led to curative
drugs, to genetic counseling, and to an unparalleled understanding of
structure–function relationships in living organisms. We look hopefully
to the development of life itself and, in concert with social–behavioral
scientists, the unraveling of the relationship between mind and brain. Despite the potential moral issues raised by the latter advances, the history
of science provides us faith that knowledge and understanding can be advanced for the benefit of humanity.

The methods for conducting scientific research that have been developed over the past centuries include the following:

- Observation
- Hypothesis
- Experimentation
- Interpretation

33

It is important to understand the nature of these methods and how each method should be used to conduct research.

Observations

There are two important roles for observations in scientific research. Initially, observations help define problems. Later, observations become a critical element in experimentation.

Medawar[84] aptly noted, "Observation is not a passive imbibition of sensory information, a mere transcription of the evidences of the senses, . . . Observation is a critical and purposive process . . ." A conscious effort has to be made to observe, and to develop a keen "eye" for things and events. This ability, new to many, comes from raising one's consciousness and developing a questioning attitude. It is fostered by thoughtful reading and a desire to comprehend and integrate knowledge. In a practical sense, the researcher constantly looks for answers to underlying questions. Biochemists, for example, automatically wonder about mechanisms of enzyme reactions, and they look for data that may provide clues. Biostatisticians question how variables were controlled in a study of the incidence of heart disease among cigarette smokers. Marine biologists question the accuracy of pH measurements in studies of the effects of acid rain on marine organisms. The thoughtful approach to observations, as exemplified, does not come easily because it is not encouraged in undergraduate school.

Undergraduates are accustomed to performing experiments exactly as described in laboratory manuals. Some students also get into the habit of studying just enough to score well on exams. Graduate education requires more thoughtful approaches and more dedication. It will take time to develop the background and perspective necessary to differentiate the old from the new, the profound from the mundane. The guidance of professors through core courses and individual research problem courses will help, but independent study and a dogged determination to be a scholar and researcher will be necessary to succeed.

Early in one's graduate career, there may be frustration because of an apparent lack of problems to solve. This feeling is common to novice researchers. It has been experienced by some of the best scientists. Herbert C. Brown, recipient of the 1979 Nobel Prize in Chemistry, reflected[19] on his early attitudes:

> In 1936 when I received my B.S. degree, I felt that organic chemistry was a relatively mature science, with essentially all of the important reactions and structures known. There appeared to be little new to be done except the working out of reaction mechanisms and the improvement of reac-

© Sidney Harris

tion yields. I now recognize that I was wrong. I have seen major reactions discovered . . . Many new structures are known.

Brown's progress as a researcher came after study and attempts to improve observations. After making meaningful observations and becoming more introspective about science, the researcher is ready to tackle the next step in the research process—developing hypotheses.

Hypotheses

A hypothesis is an imaginative preconception of a factual relationship. It comes from meaningful observations and takes the form of statements such as, "Phenomenon A is related to phenomenon B through variable C." This concept of hypotheses was not always in force. The ancient Greeks, for example, believed that hypotheses were perfect and experimentation must confirm them. During the Dark Ages a hypothesis was thought to be perfect and sufficient for gaining knowledge so long as it was blessed by theology and authority. Experimentation was unnecessary. It was not until the nineteenth century that great scientists like Louis Pasteur recommended that hypotheses be regarded as invaluable guides to action that could be discredited only by positive experimental evidence.

Hypotheses have also been referred to as theoretical generalizations which should be contrasted with empirical generalizations that are summary statements of fact. An example of an empirical generalization might be, "Chameleons assume the color of their environments." This is different from a hypothesis on chameleon behavior, as indicated below. The importance of the hypothesis in determining truth should be emphasized. Without hypotheses, the scientific process becomes a mere collection of data, and as Medawar noted,[84] "No new truth will declare itself from inside a heap of facts."

It is important to differentiate between the research hypothesis and the null hypothesis which maintains that the effect and the cause are unrelated except by chance. An original hypothesis could be that drug A is more active biologically than drug B. The null hypothesis states that there is no difference in the biological activities of the two drugs and any difference found is due to random error (chance). The null hypothesis is useful in statistics because it is more easily tested than the original hypothesis.

How are research hypotheses developed? One of the best ways is to pursue ideas through library work and to design relevant pilot experiments. Careful library research is needed to avoid "reinventing the wheel." Also, extensive reading will lead to a refinement of ideas and to the development of new concepts. Indeed, a wide range of literature—including the popular press — can be useful. In the press, however, the "what happened" *may* be accurate while the "why" and "how", as given by an inexperienced reporter, may be fantastic. Hypothetical statements should be sought out when reading, particularly in the introductory sections of articles. In particular, authors of review articles and papers from scientific meetings may speculate on the feasibility of a hypothesis where literature evidence from diverse sources points to a congruence of ideas. Antecedents to model hypotheses are listed below.

The development of hypotheses is aided by three principles:

- Method of agreement
- Method of difference
- Concomitant variation

The *method of agreement* states that, if an event with circumstances having one factor in common is repeated, the factor may be the cause of the event. Thus, it would seem obvious to hypothesize that a certain virus causes respiratory infections in mice if separate batches of the animals showed typical respiratory symptoms after repeated exposure to the suspected agent. On the other hand, the researcher can be misled by this seemingly obvious cause and effect relationship. What if the symptoms are caused by some irritant simultaneously administered with the virus? What if the viral suspensions are contaminated with infectious bacteria? These questions can be addressed only through controlled experimentation.

The *method of difference* states that, if an event is repeated with one factor but not another, the first factor is the causative agent. Looking at the earlier infectious disease problem, experiments might be conducted with two fluids: one specially treated to remove viruses and the other untreated. A lack of respiratory symptoms in animals treated with the first fluid and the regular appearance of symptoms in animals treated with the second fluid would implicate the virus as a causative agent.

The third principle, *concomitant variation*, states that if an increase in the intensity of a factor is followed by a parallel variation in effect then the factor is the cause of the event. Again, returning to the mouse experiments, different groups of animals could be subjected to increasing levels of viruses. A graded increase in the incidence and severity of respiratory symptoms would suggest a cause and effect relationship between the virus and respiratory infections.

Once a hypothesis is developed, it is necessary to determine its feasibility through pilot experimentation. This is important to conserve resources, and positive results from pilot work will help with motivation to conduct the extensive experimentation that must follow. I can recall a turning point in one student's graduate work where a set of preliminary experiments revealed the likelihood that the underlying hypothesis of the doctoral dissertation was correct. This Ph.D. work concerned the chemical transformations of the aromatic hydrocarbon *trans*-stilbene in mammals. Earlier literature had suggested that the estrogenic effect of this chemical in rabbits was caused by certain biotransformation products, yet these types of products had not been detected. The underlying hypothesis was that the products were in fact formed in rabbits and perhaps other animals but were not previously detected because of inadequate analytical methods. The pilot work required development of a simple analytical test for the expected products and an analysis of urine from a small group of rabbits administered *trans*-stilbene. Results of these preliminary experiments were positive. It took more than a year of subsequent experimentation to prove the hypothesis through careful experiments in more rabbits and two other species of animals. The feeling of accomplishment and *hope* from the pilot work, however, was of inestimable value to the student in developing the necessary perseverance to complete the doctoral work.

A caveat concerning pilot experimentation is that one can become carried away with it. Pilot experiments are not too carefully executed, and this may serve as a temptation to continue with careless work. Some students never seem to get beyond a string of less rigorously performed "preliminary experiments." Pilot experimentation has its place. It is no substitute, however, for definitive experimentation.

The reading and pilot experimentation may be done. The hypothesis must then emerge. Following are examples of hypotheses that could have been developed by three different graduate students.

- A zoologist might hypothesize:
    The American chameleon assumes the color of its environment because of unique structural changes in the molecules of its skin pigments.

Statements may have been found in the literature suggesting that chameleon skin pigment molecules are capable of undergoing structural changes. Other literature citations could have pointed to the likelihood of varying light absorption characteristics of chemical compounds resembling chameleon pigments. Pilot experiments might have indicated that changes in solution composition alter the light absorption characteristics of model pigments.

- A civil engineering scientist might hypothesize:
    Bridges made of vanadium steel are sturdier than those constructed of carbon steel.

Reports in the metallurgical literature may have contained stress–strain curves for vanadium suggesting that the atoms align and relax upon stress in a way that might prevent fatigue and cracking. Pilot experiments with the two types of steel might have suggested improved strength characteristics for vanadium steel bars.

- A psychologist might hypothesize:
    Sensory deprivation in human subjects is associated with increased alienation and is manifested as loneliness.

An article in a professional magazine for clinical psychologists might have described experiences of professionals providing services to deaf and blind clients who had no family or close friends and lived alone. A pilot survey of deaf and blind widows, and widows with normal hearing and sight, might have suggested a greater amount of loneliness in the former subjects.

Good hypotheses should be testable in a practical and a theoretical sense. The hypothesis testing should not require establishment of a new research institute or the investment of millions of dollars. Also, equipment (e.g., spectrophotometers, computers) and research tools (e.g., statistical methods, survey instruments) must be available for collecting and analyzing data that will be generated during experimentation.

The good researcher considers practical limitations. Desirable equipment for testing a hypothesis may not be available. Thought should be given to borrowing equipment or to alternative methods for achieving the same results. For example, a biologist may be aware of radioactive tracer techniques for studying a certain physiological process, but the equipment may not be available. The researcher will then require an approach which may be less convenient and more time consuming yet provide equally valid data. In summary, the hypothesis is a preconception of outcomes, it is testable, and it is the primary basis for experimentation.

Experimentation

The researcher makes things happen through experimentation! This would have been a strange idea to early scientists, who believed that discoveries were made by observing nature and waiting for events to occur in a certain juxtaposition so that truth would be revealed. In the early 1600s, Sir Francis Bacon suggested that people must make their opportunities as often as finding them.[84] Bacon's contemporary Galileo Galilei was among the first proponents of the critical experiment — one that discriminates between narrow possibilities. After Pasteur's work in the late 1800s, experiments became accepted as a test or trial of a hypothesis.

Modern experimentation is marked by quantitative measurement. As noted by Lord Kelvin[127] nearly a hundred years ago:

> When you can measure what you are speaking about and express it in numbers, you know something about it. And when you cannot measure it, when you cannot express it in numbers, your knowledge is of a meager and unsatisfactory kind. It may be the beginning of knowledge, but you have scarcely in your thought advanced to the stage of a science.

Experiments must also be subject to control. The results of experiments are never the sum total of all that is observed. Rather, a simple one-factor experiment will involve comparing the measurement of a dependent variable in the test situation to the control condition where the effect of this variable is small or nil. The result is the difference between the two conditions — *experiment* minus *control*. More complicated (multiple-factor) experiments can be performed to measure the effects of more than one dependent variable. Suitable controls, however, must be instituted for each.

Good experimentation is marked by methodical planning and execution. The planning must include considerations such as: numbers of experimental subjects and controls, treatment conditions, and methods of analysis, including statistical tests. The civil engineering scientist alluded to earlier, for example, would consider several factors in designing experiments to test his or her hypothesis that bridges made of vanadium steel are sturdier than those constructed of carbon steel. Initially, samples of the two types of steel would have to be obtained and tests performed to confirm their composition. This would require some type of chemical analysis. The steels would then be used to construct model bridges which could be subjected to stress–strain measurements. All equipment would have to be calibrated to determine the accuracy (how close actual values are to theoretical values) and precision (the variability in repeated measurements) of the measurement steps. The conditions for the stress–strain determinations, such as temperature, period of stress, degree of stress, and points of stress, would be defined. The measurements obtained would be treated statistically to determine possible differences between the bridge types.

The design of experiments is a science unto itself. Good execution, on the other hand, requires practice much like that of a concert pianist. It can be thought of as the "art of experimentation." Young researchers often harbor the fantasy that a few offhand observations and experiments will bring success. This comes under the heading of "get-rich-quick" schemes that are commonplace in our society and undoubtedly responsible for the popularity of various forms of gambling. As noted earlier, experimentation provides little instant gratification. It takes commitment and hard work to achieve results.

One way to improve execution in experimentation is to attempt model experiments or to repeat work of a predecessor. Good research advisors know this and will often initially assign some of the completed work of a former graduate student. This serves two purposes: it helps develop technique, and it provides an additional opportunity to test the results of the previous investigation. Alternatively, a newly proposed experiment may be tried initially with a simpler system—one in which the prediction of success is high. This is common practice for organic chemists who plan the synthesis of a complex natural product. After inspecting the target molecule, the chemist proposes ways of constructing it in stages from less and less complex starting materials. The resulting total synthesis scheme may require more than 10 steps, many of which may not occur readily and may involve the use of rare starting materials. In these instances, a model reaction with less complex compounds may be performed to determine the potential usefulness of a proposed chemical reaction step. If the reaction is successful, further reactions with the same model compounds may be performed to improve yields. When conditions have been optimized, the parallel reaction is run with the rare starting materials.

A successful approach to difficult experimental problems is to break them up into several smaller experiments and to complete the work in parts. The "parts" are then ordered through sub-hypotheses and tackled so the easiest experiments are performed first. In the *trans*-stilbene problem, for example, the work beyond the pilot experiments was subdivided. After developing methods for detecting metabolites in urine, additional analytical procedures were devised to determine the concentrations of metabolites in urine. Procedures were also developed to confirm the structural formulae of metabolites. Evidence for the proposed metabolites in rabbits encouraged experiments in two other species of mammals, mice and guinea pigs.

Quantitative analysis of the metabolites in rabbits, mice, and guinea pigs indicated problems with mass balance calculations. That is, the total amounts of metabolites formed did not match the amounts of *trans*-stilbene administered. This prompted hypotheses about alternative pathways of biotransformation and excretion that were subsequently studied by other students. Thus, results of experiments led to new hypotheses which in turn led to new experiments. One dissertation problem led to others. This is the nature of scientific research.

Like all research, the *trans*-stilbene work was often difficult and tedious. It was important, therefore, for the student to order the experiments so that the easiest steps were accomplished first. Sometimes one hears a statement like, "If I can accomplish the most difficult experiment first, then all the rest will be easy." This is most often a nonsensical idea that can lead to unnecessary failure and despair. Usually it is more sensible to progress from easier to harder experiments, though pilot experiments of more difficult stages of the research are frequently helpful as noted earlier.

Writing out protocols can help the beginning researcher with first experiments. These strict sets of directions for experiments list details on materials and methods. The psychologist working with widowed subjects, for example, might prepare a protocol for a major experiment by addressing the following questions:

1. How many widows and widowers will be needed in the study and control groups?
2. How will the subjects be recruited and how will informed consent be obtained?
3. What instrument(s) (questionnaire) will be used in the study?
4. Under what conditions will the questionnaire be administered?
5. If the questionnaire is mailed to subjects, how will return rates be improved?
6. How will subject confidentiality be protected during and after the study?
7. How will the questionnaire responses be scored and the results analyzed?
8. What level of significance is necessary to prove the hypothesis?

The complete protocol would be reviewed with the psychology student's advisor prior to implementation. Since it involves human subjects, the study would also require review by the human subjects research committee of the university.

If the psychology student found that alienation and loneliness were statistically significantly greater in the sensory deprived subjects, questions for new hypotheses might arise such as:

1. Is the difference age dependent? Are similar differences apparent in younger subjects?
2. Are there differences in alienation between men and women?
3. What are the effects of institutionalization?
4. Are the same differences observed in people who were never married?

Thus, research leads to research. Proof of one hypothesis leads to broader and broader hypotheses and theories.

The best stimulus for achieving goals is initial success. Indeed, until something of worth is accomplished, there may be frequent crises of incentive. Dedication is particularly necessary at first to achieve some measure of success later. Once new researchers have one or two satisfying accomplishments behind them, future experimental efforts (even with unavoidable failures) can be faced more optimistically. After students have reached a certain stage of accomplishment, then and only then are they able to begin each day with the thought, "Even if everything goes wrong today, I have something to fall back on." This feeling of confidence enables researchers to apply themselves effectively, and, inevitably, other successful experiments follow. This feeling also inspires greater and greater confidence.

A fantasy that plagues new researchers is success by chance. That is, some unexpected event will occur that is highly significant. Chance or serendipity does have a role to play in scientific discoveries, as indicated previously. It only works, however, for the keen and experienced researcher. It has been claimed that the discovery of penicillin by Sir Alexander Fleming resulted from the inadvertent contamination of a microbiological culture he was studying. Without the insight of a knowledgeable scientist, however, the contaminated plates might well have been discarded and the discovery of the first antibiotic would have been delayed.

To allow for serendipity and to properly engage in experimentation, one has to be open minded. Also, one must not become so wedded to a hypothesis as to be blinded to the truth. Ira Remson, the first chairman of the department of chemistry at Johns Hopkins University, once noted[28]:

> Great harm has been done chemistry, and probably every other branch of knowledge, by unwarranted speculation, and every one who has looked into the matter knows how extremely difficult it is to emancipate one's self from the influence of a plausible hypothesis even when it can be shown that it is not in accordance with the facts.

Experimentation must be carried out in the spirit that results will be accepted and interpreted according to how they happen.

Interpretation

Interpretation is developing meaning from data. As emphasized earlier, the data are developed from experimentation that results from testing a hypothesis. During the initial interpretative processes it must be determined whether the data fit the underlying hypothesis. Approaches to this include: statistics, tabulating and plotting data, library work and in-

Table 1 Statistics texts and software

Type of Volume	Reference
Text	Cochran, W. G., and G. W. Snedecor. 1980. Statistical methods, 7th ed. Iowa State University Press, Ames
Text	Cox, D. R. 1958. Planning of experiments. Wiley, New York
Text	Hays, W. L. 1981. Statistics, 3rd ed. Holt, Rinehart and Winston, New York
Text	Kirk, R. E. 1982. Experimental design: procedures for the behavioral sciences, 2nd ed. Brooks/Cole, Monterey, Calif.
Text	Olson, S. 1976. Ideas and data: the process and practice of social research. Dorsey, Homewood, Ill.
Text	Remington, R. D., and M. A. Schork. 1970. Statistics with applications to the biological and medical sciences. Prentice Hall, Englewood Cliffs, N.J.
Text	Sokal, R. R., and F. J. Rohlf. 1981. Biometry. The principles and practice of statistics in biological research, 2nd ed. Freeman, New York
Text and software	Bevington, P. R. 1969. Data reduction and error analysis for the physical sciences. McGraw-Hill, New York
Text and software	BMD: Biomedical computer programs. 1973. W. J. Dixon (ed.). University of California Press, Berkeley.
Text and software	Nie, N. H., C. H. Hull, J. G. Jenkins, K. Steinbrenner, and D. H. Bent. 1975. Statistical package for the social sciences (SPSS), 2nd ed. McGraw-Hill, New York.
Text and software	Ryan, T. A., B. L. Joiner, and B. F. Ryan. 1976. Minitab student handbook. Duxbury Press, North Scituate, Mass.

trospection, and discussions with an advisor and other faculty or students.

Statistical analyses help in making objective judgments about differences in data sets and degrees of significance of differences. Statistics courses are important additions to most graduate students' programs. Additionally, the basic texts and statistics software listed in Table 1 are recommended.

Tabulating and plotting data are also useful ways of seeing relationships in data. Indeed, most advisors will recommend these treatments for written reports and as aids in formal research conferences.

Interpretation is made easier by library work and reflective thinking. One cannot hold to a timetable at this stage. When insight won't come, it is helpful to "forget" the problem for a while. A period of incubation may subsequently be followed by illumination. This spark, referred to as "aha! insight,"[53] may come at unusual times such as when traveling, when dozing or waking, or even during times of personal hygiene or evacuation. Jaynes[65] referred to these times as the three B's—the bus, the bed, and the bath.

As noted earlier, Kekulé first imagined an answer to the benzene problem while dozing on a bus. Einstein was frequently inspired while shaving.[65] Karl Folkers has described the traveling incident when he first became convinced of a structural formula for penicillin: "On the train from Chicago to Madison, I sat there, looking out the window, . . . As I reviewed the evidence in my mind about the beta-lactam formulas, they sounded pretty good . . . It was on that trip that for the first time in my participation in the penicillin program, that I really took the beta-lactam seriously."[115] Walt Rostow[112] has related the unusual timing of the inspiration for his recent book on economics: "At 3:00 a.m. on the morning of December 15, 1982, when sleep was light, I got up and outlined this book in just about the form that it now appears." Other effective researchers have experienced similar occurrences, and they go no place without pencil and pad. These "instruments" are even kept on the night table. Researchers develop some of their best ideas while traveling to and from scientific meetings. Oddly enough, as the astronauts had to leave the earth to see its grandeur for the "first time," the solutions to local problems are often found by "leaving" them. New researchers should be aware of the potential influence of the three B's on insight. This will help tremendously.

Once an interpretation for data is developed, it must be subjected to the scrutiny of others. Here, other graduate students and certainly an advisor are important. Ultimately, research results and interpretations will be presented at scientific meetings and prepared for publication in peer-reviewed journals. This self-correcting process is essential to science.

The successful researcher lives a life of observation, hypothesis, experimentation, and interpretation. This requires integrity and a sense of fair play that are discussed in the next chapter.

Chapter 6

Ethics and the Scientist

*We are a scientific civilization . . . that means
a civilization in which knowledge and its
integrity are crucial.*

—Jacob Bronowski

The needs of creative scientists are best served in a free and democratic society. It should be no surprise, therefore, that the most significant work in science and research during the past 50 years has occurred in the United States and Western Europe. These achievements would have been impossible without intellectual honesty and social responsibility.

Intellectual honesty is the guardian of the integrity of science. It is a necessity for the growth of researchers and scholars, and it is not easily nurtured. As noted by Reid,[106] we naturally wish to make the best appearances possible. Indeed, there is little hope for anyone's self-esteem without an inherent desire to look good to peers. Unfortunately, this ambition can lead to concealment and pretentiousness. Researchers are tempted to make experiments appear more thorough than they actually were, mention experimental precautions that were not taken or were not always adhered to, and describe a more perfected methodology than was actually used. Graduating students are tempted to make résumés reflect work that has not been done or to distort the importance of achievements. These temptations may come from a desire to make the results and accomplishments appear better than they really are, or they may arise when results are not as expected. Novice researchers may not understand experimental errors and variance, or how these factors are manifest in different kinds of studies. For example, analytical chemists may expect precision errors of ±1% when determining the sodium chloride content of an electrolyte solution. Clinical pharmacologists, in contrast, commonly observe ±50% variations in responses of patients to drugs. It is important to learn about experimental errors and variations that should be expected in one's area of research. This knowledge can be obtained through experimental methods courses and through guidance from an advisor and role models.

Students are also tempted into dishonesty by a desire to please a demanding research advisor or to get away with a hoax. Such thoughts should not be harbored for a minute because they can lead to disaster.

Most students are above cheating because of moral convictions. Aside from morality, however, cheating is foolish because of the likelihood of detection. Cheating requires predicting the outcome of series of experiments which cannot be done by the best scientists. Even if one "succeeds" in fooling people temporarily, the chances of getting caught are great because of the scientific method. As noted earlier, advisors often assign previously completed work to novice researchers for experimental practice. If fudged results are published without such a check, attempts at replication are likely by researchers in other laboratories. Thus, the cheater is doomed to failure.

In a practical sense, cheating takes the fun out of research. Half of the thrill of research is in not knowing answers which are subsequently discovered. Making up or fudging data destroys the excitement of discovery.

The cheater is also alienated from the scientific community, whose members hate cheaters. Everyone knows of criminals who seemingly "get away with murder"; but criminals at least have friends—if not in society then in the penitentiary. Researchers who cheat have no friends, no colleagues to console them.

Recent cases of fraudulent experimentation in the biomedical research community emphasize the need for constant vigilance against intellectual dishonesty. The scientific world has no patience with it because of both altruistic and self-serving reasons. Regarding the latter, the self-correcting nature of science is violated by fraud. As indicated earlier, hypotheses are never absolutely proven. Each series of experiments builds upon the work of predecessors. Indeed, it is not in the nature of scientific research that investigators make sudden violent discoveries. This is the stuff of science fiction—not real life. Rather, sudden or seemingly unexpected discoveries are results of findings of many sequential studies by different investigators. This is also why discoveries occur simultaneously in laboratories around the world. The importance of one investigator's work to that of another cannot be overemphasized. Thus, if falsehood is introduced along the way, enormous difficulty is created, and valuable time and resources are required to correct the course.

One additional point needs to be made about honesty in scientific research. Science is not like politics or the law. The rules on honesty are

© Sidney Harris

"What's most depressing is the realization that everything
we believe will be disproved in a few years."

absolute—there can be no compromises, no plea bargaining, and no saving face. Scientists must be dogmatic on honesty to protect the integrity of science and their pursuit of truth.

Intellectual honesty in experimentation can be fostered through the proper preparation of research notebooks. Recording results soon after observations are made is an important tactic. Another healthy practice is to voluntarily submit work to the scrutiny of others. This may be done by volunteering for seminars and for presentations at research group conferences held by an advisor. Subjecting work to critical evaluations provides additional motives for "staying honest." This is one function of the peer review system in science. Also, frequent evaluations help everyone uncover the truth and help lower one's sensitivity to criticism.

Dishonesty in science transcends laboratory work. Plagiarism and deception in the preparation and publication of manuscripts are also practices that must be avoided. It is important to cite others' work properly and to obtain permission for the use of published material. Sentences or phrases lifted verbatim from others' work must be placed in quotations and the source cited. Large sections of materials such as paragraphs, tables, or figures can be used only after receiving permission from their copyright holder(s).

A copyright is a right of protection or monopoly for a piece of literature or art, and it exists whether or not an application has been filed with the Register of Copyrights. The terms of copyrights vary with circumstances, but for a newly created work, the term is usually the author's life plus 50 years. The permission to use copyrighted or other printed materials must be obtained in writing from the copyright owner by using a letter with format similar to the one indicated in Figure 5. Ethics also requires that courtesy approval be sought from the author of material to be reproduced, even if the author has assigned the copyright to someone else. Permission for cartoons may require a letter to a publishing syndicate, addresses for which are found in *Literary Market Place*. [76]

Other dishonest practices of authors include duplicative publication, submission of papers or manuscripts to more than one journal, and premature submission of abstracts for presentation at scientific meetings. Everyone is aware of the "publish or perish" adage which reflects the pressure applied by administrators to scholars and researchers to produce. The pressure is often real. Additionally, competition for grants and contracts hinges on the quality and quantity of published works. Unfortunately, the need for quantity may be exaggerated. Melvin Gibson, a professor at Washington State University, is fond of saying that "deans can count but can't read." In reality, thoughtful faculty and peer review groups do evaluate publication quality. Moreover, shoddy publication practices tend to discount the good work produced by a scholar.

Abelson[2] points out that duplicate publication: hinders communi-

Address of Copyright
Owner or Author of
Printed Material

Dear Sir/Madam:

I request permission to use published material for which I understand you own the copyright.

The copyrighted material I wish to use is as follows:

_____

My use of this material is to have it published in the following journal (book, etc.):

_____

The publisher will be: _____

Proper acknowledgment of copyright owner and date will be given in the work.

If you approve of my request, please indicate your permission by signing on the line below and returning this letter to me in the enclosed self-addressed stamped envelope. I enclose a duplicate copy of this letter for your records.

Thank you for your cooperation in this matter.

                                   Sincerely,

Date: _____

Permission Granted:

_____
Signature of copyright owner or agent

Figure 5 Letter format for obtaining permission to publish copyrighted and other printed materials.

cations between scientists, steals time from reviewers and editorial staffs, and creates excessive costs for government, libraries, and scientific societies. It is in everyone's interest to avoid excessive publication, and stiff penalties (e.g., boycotting of authors for three years) for attempts at duplicate publication have now been instituted by at least three prestigious American journals.[2] Similar future penalties are likely for simultaneous submissions of works to other journals.

Besides being dishonest and wasteful of editorial efforts, simultaneous manuscript submittals are potentially embarrassing. What does one do if two journals accept a manuscript at once? It is agonizing to think of the fractured conversation that would result. Does one lie about the dual submission? That creates double jeopardy. The best route is the one followed by most scientists. You plod from one journal to another as necessary to get good work published.

Investigators have been known to submit meeting abstracts of work yet to be done. The time between submittal and presentation requires a scramble to complete the "proposed" study with the hope that it turns out as predicted. This anxiety-laden behavior is dishonest and is discouraged. Furthermore, there often isn't enough time to finish the work before the meeting. One can wind up having to withdraw the paper, which is an embarrassment to the author and her or his department.

To this point, the impact of dishonesty on science and the scientific community has been considered. But what about society? Are there obligations here? Actually, there are unselfish and selfish motives that should make researchers consider seriously their responsibilities to society. In so doing, acknowledgment is given to the substantial support to science made through federal and state governments. If science's standards call for impeccable honesty, then society will hold researchers accountable for nothing less. In a practical sense, scientists cannot afford to be dishonest.

Another aspect of societal responsibility stems from the scientist's need for free inquiry. If science's public image is tarnished significantly, more and more controls will be placed on researchers' activities because of their ties to government. Scientists must retain their freedom by voluntarily policing their ranks.

Researchers' obligations to society also include a willingness to explain their research to the lay public. It has been suggested that, if you can't explain your research to your mother, you don't understand it yourself. This standard is important if we are to continue to have the sympathetic support generally given to scientists by the public.

The sense of social responsibility required of researchers and scholars is self-reinforcing. As contributions are made, a need is experienced to contribute further. In a qualitative sense, there is a desire to work on more and more important projects. In turn, the more important proposals are the ones most likely to receive public support.

The previous chapters provide background on what is expected of new graduate students as they become experienced researchers. It is now time to consider additional activities that improve effectiveness in research. The first of these is library and literature work, which is covered in the next chapter.

Chapter 7

Library and Literature Work

*. . . as important as computer literacy will be in
the brave new world, special powers will always
belong to those who can read and write well.*
— MARIE JEAN LEDERMAN

Literature work is important to the growth of scholars and researchers. Without reading and library skills, the writing talents that are crucial to experimental work cannot be developed. Unfortunately, many baccalaureate programs underemphasize reading and writing. This handicaps beginning graduate students.

Reading helps reseachers by:

- stimulating ideas
- improving knowledge
- avoiding duplication of previously accomplished work
- reinforcing or refuting hypotheses

Reading also influences commitments. Bogardus noted[13] that Luther Burbank, the renowned American naturalist, ". . . based his whole natural world on a new foundation" after reading Darwin. Burbank described his reading experience as ". . . the turning point in my life work." I remember one student whose decision to pursue graduate work in pharmaceutical chemistry was made after reading an early edition of Adrian Albert's *Selective Toxicity.*[3]

Reading also helps develop self-esteem by improving capabilities and confirming difficulties experienced by others. As reading habits become stronger, perspectives develop that improve abilities to contribute to research and its attendant discussions. This promotes respect from peers and causes an inner sense of accomplishment. Once committed to reading, ways should be sought to improve one's abilities to search, evaluate, and keep up with the literature.

Searching the Literature

There are few ideas that have not already occurred in some way to researchers. Even wholly novel ideas have their parallels in the literature. Before starting an investigation, therefore, it is important to know about previous findings. During subsequent experimental work, literature searches will help to uncover information that may help explain observations and confirm or refute hypotheses. The searches may be simple or complex; they may or may not involve use of computerized systems. Most searches will require the use of libraries and consultations with librarians.

Using the Library

The word library comes from the Latin, *liber*, for book. Libraries, however, are more than mere collections of books. They are depositories for many types of materials (see Table 2) and they are instructional centers. Universities employ librarians who are willing and able to help researchers with the most complex problems. Indeed, some library professionals recommend that researchers choose a librarian just as they would choose an advisor. It is important, however, to have knowledge of the systems for filing and retrieving materials.

Many universities have a handbook on library services for faculty and students. The handbook may have a map describing the type and location of libraries on campus. Having obtained a copy of the handbook, one should locate the main graduate library. Librarians in this facility organize tours and slide-tape or film programs that will help with the use of campus libraries.

Every campus has at least one library with a card catalog that lists holdings for the entire campus. This is important to know if library research is being done on a topic that transcends the holdings in branch libraries.

Card catalogs are organized in three ways:

- Author
- Subject
- Title

Headings used in the subject index, as exemplified in Table 3, are listed in the *Library of Congress—Subject Headings*[75] which is usually located near the card catalog. The subject headings index also lists related topics and seemingly related topics that are not used for indexing. Books and periodicals located through use of the card catalog are shelved according to the Library of Congress or Dewey Decimal System. The advan-

Table 2 Holdings of university libraries

Main Group	Items
Books — general collection[a]	Fiction Non-fiction: textbooks, monographs (books written on a single topic), biographies and autobiographies
Periodicals and newspapers[b]	Current issues Past issues[c]
Reference books[b]	Dictionaries and encyclopedias Periodical indexes Annual reviews Handbooks Atlases (books containing maps, tables, charts, or plates) Gazetteer (geographical dictionary)
Pamphlets and clippings[b]	Classified pamphlets[d] Government publications[e]
Vertical file materials[b]	Clippings from newspapers Small pamphlets
Audiovisual materials[b]	Pictures Maps Slides, filmstrips, motion picture films, video-tapes Microfilms,[f] microcards,[g] microfiches[h] Disc, tape, and cassette recordings Globes Models Specimens[i]

[a] Circulating material.

[b] Non-circulating materials.

[c] Bound volumes or on microfilm reels, cassettes, microcards, or microfiches.

[d] Pamphlets filed with general collection of books.

[e] Publications of the U.S. Government Printing Office.

[f] Reels of 35- or 16-mm film with contents of journals or out-of-print books. Require a special viewing machine.

[g] Opaque cards with microprint. Require a different viewer than that used for viewing microfilms or microfiches.

[h] Card-sized sheet of film containing many images. An entire issue of a journal may be published on a single microfiche which must be read with a special viewer.

[i] Historically important artifacts.

(Taken in part from D. N. Dutta, Libraries and their use, pp. 21 and 70–74, World Press Private, Calcutta, India, 1975. Reprinted by permission of the publisher.)

Table 3 Examples of Library of Congress subject headings[a]

Main Heading		Sub-Headings
Neuroses	*sa*[b]	Depression, Mental
		Inferiority complex
		Medicine, Psychosomatic
		Mentally ill
		Nail biting
		Neurotics
		Obsessive-compulsive neurosis
		Occupational neuroses
		Phobias
		Psychological manifestation of general diseases
		Psychoses
		Traumatic neuroses
		particular neuroses, e.g., Anxiety, Hysteria
	x[c]	Psychoneuroses
	xx[d]	Insanity
		Psychology, Pathological Psychoses
—Diagnosis	*sa*	Personality tests
	xx	Psychological tests

[a] Taken from *Library of Congress—Subject Headings*. [75]
[b] *sa* = see also; indicates a reference to a related topic or subordinate topic.
[c] *x* = expression not itself used as a heading for neuroses.
[d] *xx* = related or broader heading used elsewhere with *sa* notation to neuroses.

tage of both systems is that books are grouped according to subjects. Thus, if a particular title is sought and found to be checked out, other titles of interest will be found near the spot for the missing book.

A lack of subject cards for a particular topic in the card catalog indicates no holdings in the library. This does not mean, however, that no books exist on the topic. It may simply mean that the library has a deficiency. To locate relevant books, one can consult bibliographic listings such as *Books in Print*, [15] *Scientific and Technical Books and Serials in Print*, [114] *Medical Books and Serials in Print*, [86] or *Sources of Information in the Social Sciences*. [136] Books discovered by this process may be available through other university or state libraries.

Recent books may be a good start for a literature search. Library work in a new area, however, may require starting at a more fundamental level. This can be done through scientific encyclopedias, dictionaries, and handbooks as listed in literature guides. [26,29,81,82,111] A guide to U.S. Government publications [111] is also available.

Another way to begin a literature search is to find a good recent review article. The semiannual *Index to Scientific Reviews* (ISR) [63] can be

Table 4 Indexes to the scientific literature

Field	Index Title	Publisher
Bioengineering	Bioengineering Abstracts	Engineering Index, 345 E. 47th St., New York, NY 10017
Biological sciences	Biological Abstracts	BIOSIS, 2100 Arch St., Philadelphia, PA 19103-1399
Chemistry	Chemical Abstracts	Chemical Abstracts Service, P.O. Box 3012, Columbus, OH 43210
	Current Abstracts of Chemistry	Institute for Scientific Information, 3501 Market St., Philadelphia, PA 19104
Dental medicine	Index to Dental Literature	American Dental Association, 211 E. Chicago Ave., Chicago, IL 60611
Engineering	Engineering Index	Engineering Index (see above)
Environmental sciences	Environmental Abstracts	Environmental Information Center, 292 Madison Ave., New York, NY 10017
	Pollution Abstracts	Data Courier Inc., 620 S. 5th St., Louisville, KY 40202
	Safety Science	Cambridge Scientific Abstracts, 6611 Kenilworth Ave., Riverdale, MD 20840
Medicine	Index Medicus	National Library of Medicine, Office of Inquiries and Publications, 8600 Rockville Pike, Bethesda, MD 20209
	Excerpta Medica[a]	Excerpta Medica, P.O. Box 1126, Amsterdam, The Netherlands
	Psychopharmacology Abstracts	National Institute of Mental Health, 5600 Fishers Lane, Rockville, MD 20857
Nursing	International Nursing Index	American Journal of Nursing Co., 555 W. 57th St., New York, NY 10019
	Cumulative Index to Nursing and Allied Health Literature	Cumulative Index in Nursing and Allied Health Literature, P.O. Box 871, Glendale, CA 91209
Pharmacy	International Pharmaceutical Abstracts	American Society of Hospital Pharmacy, 4630 Montgomery Ave., Bethesda, MD 20814

Table 4 (Continued)

Field	Index Title	Publisher
Psychology	Psychological Abstracts	American Psychological Association, 1200 Seventeenth St., N.W., Washington, DC 20036
Sociology	Sociological Abstracts	Sociological Abstracts, Inc., P.O. Box 22206, San Diego, CA 92122
	Social Sciences Citation Index[b]	Institute for Scientific Information (see above)
Various fields	Conference Papers Index[c]	Data Courier, Inc. (see above)
	Index to Scientific and Technical Proceedings	Institute for Scientific Information (see above)
	Comprehensive Dissertation Index[d]	Xerox University Microfilms, 300 N. Zeeb Road, Ann Arbor, MI 48103

[a] Includes sections on forensic science, and environmental health and pollution control.

[b] Organized the same as *Science Citation Index* (see Table 5).

[c] Index of papers presented at worldwide scientific and technical meetings since 1973.

[d] Abstracts nearly all U.S. and many foreign dissertations. Most dissertations abstracted are available in complete form for a fee.

used to locate one or more of the greater than 25,000 review articles published yearly. Review journals and annuals are available in most disciplines, and they can be located through the card catalog. The potential worth of reviews can be judged from the following criteria:

- Is the author(s) an acknowledged expert?
- Are the scope and purpose clearly stated?
- How many years are covered?
- Are the references up to date?
- Does the author critically evaluate published material?
- Is the review well organized?
- Does the author suggest possible future directions for the research being reviewed?

Searching the Periodical Literature

Few literature searches are complete without a search of the periodical literature. The card catalog and library serials listing will provide

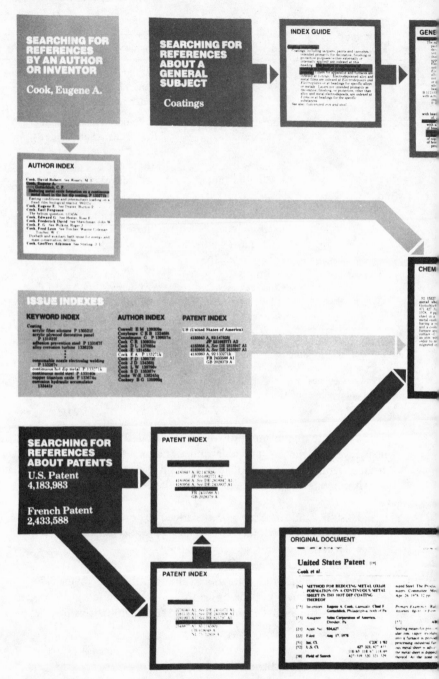

Figure 6. Scheme for using *Chemical Abstracts*. (From poster, Searching CA, Chemical Abstracts Service, American Chemical Society, Columbus, Ohio. Reprinted by permission of the publisher.)

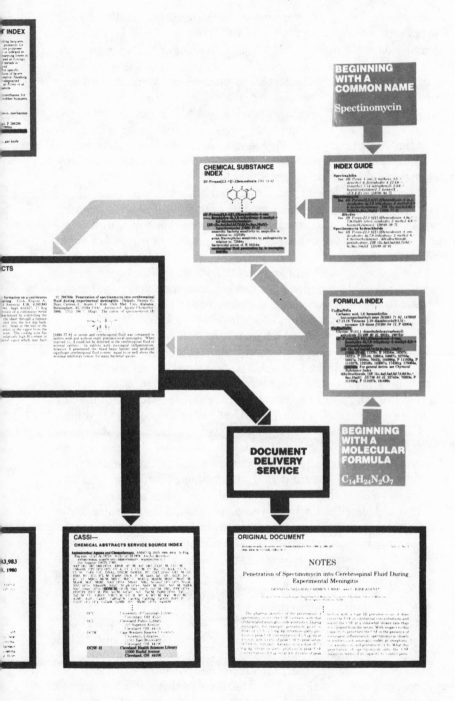

leads to journals that publish articles in particular fields. Finding articles on specific topics will require a search of one or more standard indexes. Depending on the circumstances, either a manual or a computer-based search may be conducted.

Before tackling the periodical literature, consider whether an exhaustive or a narrow search is needed. Are references needed only in English, or must literature in all languages be found? What period of time must the search cover? These are important questions if a computer search is contemplated because few computer data bases cover literature before 1970. After considering these points, decide on the indexes and computer-based systems that are necessary (see below).

Once the topic for the search has been chosen, develop a list of related terms and key words, using the *Library of Congress—Subject Headings*, scientific dictionaries, and descriptions found in one of the indexes listed in Table 4. As the search is conducted, be open to new terms or phrases that are encountered. Also, be aware of terms that may have been used in earlier volumes of an index but are dropped in later volumes. Date the previously developed key word list, and add dates to new terms or phrases as the search proceeds. It is also wise to keep a log of volumes searched to prevent duplication of effort.

The indexes listed in Table 4 have similar formats and directions for use. Volumes with topics and subtopics listed alphabetically are consulted initially to obtain numbered entries. The numbered entries are located in other volumes that contain the full bibliographic references and usually an abstract of the paper. The bibliographic reference consists of the title of the paper, name(s) of author(s), title of the journal or book, volume and page numbers of the article, and the date. A scheme for the use of *Chemical Abstracts* is given in Figure 6. Other standard abstracts (e.g., *Biological Abstracts, Index Medicus*) are used similarly, and directions for the use of indexes and lists of periodicals abstracted (with abbreviations) are given in volumes that should be available on tables near the indexes. Also, Huth[62] described a step-by-step- procedure for searching *Index Medicus.*

A periodical search should begin with the latest volumes and proceed backwards. As the search continues, breaks in the effort should be found to review original literature reports. This helps to alleviate the tedium of searching. Also, the intermittent reading may lead to important references through bibliographic citations.

Beginning graduate students have a tendency to think that all literature searchers are exhaustive. Actually, there are many types of searches. Some are aimed simply at finding a specific fact or precedent for an experimental result; other searches are extensive. With experience, researchers develop the intuition of a detective, and they use a combination of traditional searching routines and selective forays into the literature to

Table 5 *Science Citation Index* and its use

Sub-Index	Description and Use
Source Index[a,b]	Alphabetically arranged author index with entries including: names of all authors, language code, full paper title, book number (book titles listed in separate section), or journal name, volume, and issue, inclusive page numbers, year of publication, number of references listed in work, and full mailing address of first author.
Citation Index[a]	Alphabetically arranged first-author index with entries including: author and abbreviated citation that has been cited during previous year; abbreviated citations including first authors and their works which cite author's work listed. Full citations of author cited and authors citing work are available through *Source Index*.
Permuterm Subject Index[a]	Significant terms and combinations from titles of works published during year covered with author references. Relevant works are found through first author's name in *Source Index*.

[a] Issued annually and containing references to >500,000 papers and other editorial items covered in *Science Citation Index*.

[b] Also contains an index which permits location of authors by their organizational affiliation, and a section for locating anonymously authored papers through publications in which they are cited.

uncover needed information. The experienced researcher also learns to associate particular types of research with specific researchers around the world. This is the basis for the usefulness of *Science Citation Index* (SCI), which is described in Table 5.

Despite unfamiliarity with scientists in a particular field, SCI allows one to search backward or forward for citations to a key researcher's work. This novel searching method can lead to quick answers to specific questions. SCI is also useful in reviewing the contributions of researchers and the quality of journals. It is generally recognized that publication in prestigious journals favors frequent citation.

The indexes listed in Table 4 can be used to locate original research reports, review articles, and abstracts of U.S. and some foreign patents. Full U.S. patents can be reviewed at one of many libraries in the United States that have been listed by Maizell.[81] Alternatively, patents can be searched through standard data bases (see Appendix 1). Copies of patents can be purchased for one dollar each from the Commissioner of Patents and Trademarks, Washington, D.C. 20231. Copies of most foreign patents may be obtained from the same source for 30 cents per page, photocopy. Foreign patents are also available at modest prices from two domestic sources: either Air-Mail Patent Service, Box 2232, Arlington, Va. 22202, or IFI Plenum/Data Co., 2001 Jefferson Davis Highway, Arlington, Va. 22202.

Computerized searches can save time and effort, and many data bases are now available, as indicated in Appendix 1. These data bases are on-line systems that require interaction with a large central computer via telephone hookup.

Besides time savings, computer-based searches work through the iterative development of search terms and phrases which involves linking and coordination of terms based on the developing success of the search. This requires cooperation with a library specialist who may actually perform the search. Universities have rules for engaging these specialists. There may also be procedures for payment of computer connect time, communication, and off-line printing charges.

It is wise to work closely with a library specialist to maximize the effectiveness of a computer-based search. Agreement should be reached on the list of topics and key words to be used. Also, a list should be made of all possible abbreviations or key words to be used during the search. This improves coverage and decreases the possibility of missing important references.

Evaluating the Literature

It is important to maximize the benefit of reading research papers. This can be accomplished in several ways.

Writing in science is compact — it is composed of short phrases and sentences. This requires thoughtful reading — digestion of all words. As noted in the last chapter, time must be taken to examine the quality of experimental work, to challenge mentally hypotheses and conclusions, and to contemplate the need for further experimentation. Speed reading is useful in scanning journals or abstracts for items of interest, but slow methodical reading is necessary for serious study.

One's memory is improved by coordinating self-imposed reading assignments with progress in research. Information needs should be anticipated by planning experiments as far ahead as possible and by developing reading schedules. An understanding of the literature also improves during the preparation of reports and papers. Deadlines for writing projects create some "dither" which seems to improve one's ability to learn.

Reading effectiveness is also improved by note taking. This can be done in several ways. For personally owned books, selective highlighting

Bibliography Card.

CT
275
C3
W35
Call No.

Library:
Suzzallo

1. Author __Wall__   __Joseph__   __Frazier__
          Last Name   First Name   M.I.

2. Title and Subtitle __Andrew Carnegie__

3. Publisher __Oxford Univ. Press__ ____ City __N.Y.__ ____ State ____

4. Periodical/Series _____

5. Class: Book __✓__; Periodical/Reference__; Bulletin/Yearbook__; Report/Survey__;
Newspaper__; Other_____

6. Year __70__ 7. Month____ 8. Date/Daily____ 9. Vol.#____ 10. Pages/Columns __1137__

11. Remarks __Excellent biography; descriptions of A.C.'s complicated business dealings unusually skillful. Not much on Carnegie Institution of Washington. Does confirm what other sources say about A.C.'s personality and methods.__

Content Card.

__Carnegie__
   Topic

Page	
	Reference Wall, A. Carnegie
861	"of all Carnegie's philanthropic trusts, the Carnegie Institution of Washington received the least amount of criticism from the lay public and the academic world."

Figure 7. Bibliography and content cards used in note taking. (From D. Madsen, *Successful dissertations and theses. A guide to graduate student research from proposal to completion*, pp. 64 and 65. Jossey-Bass, San Francisco, 1983. Reprinted by permission of the publisher.)

or underlining is useful to emphasize important words or sentences. I also like to write in margins and to catalog the notes in order of appearance on the end papers at the front of the book. The latter practice is helpful for long-term projects where notes and highlights may sit for years before being consulted.

For library books and journals, a note-taking system should be devised. Many writers recommend a dual-card system for notes. This includes bibliography and content cards (see Figure 7) which can be printed in different colors. Both cards can be 3 × 5 inches or 5 × 8 inches. Some authors prefer the smaller size for bibliography cards and the larger size for content cards to accommodate more writing.

Note cards should be written in ink rather than pencil to prevent smudging during shuffling. Filing by subject is most effective for subsequent retrieval of information (see below).

Notes can also be taken, organized, and retrieved by microcomputer. The *Sci-Mate*™ *Personal Data Manager* software[54,55] offered by the Institute for Scientific Information (ISI) is designed for on-line and off-line use with microcomputers such as an Apple II. Sci-Mate™ is a menu-driven "user-friendly" system (i.e., a special computer language is not necessary to use the program) that can be adopted easily and allows searches for entries regardless of how many times a day the data base is updated or changed. The software also incorporates Boolean logic which allows searches using combined descriptors. For example, a physics researcher may initially want a listing of all entries where *fission* is used as a subject. This could subsequently be restricted to entires where both *fission* and *fusion* are used as descriptors. Finally, the search could be narrowed to *fission–fusion* entries from a particular journal or laboratory.

Sci-Mate™ can be used to search a data base broadly by calling up all entries with a particular prefix. For example, the prefix bronch_____ used with a biomedical researcher's data base might turn up entries with key words such as bronchiole, bronchial asthma, bronchoscopic, etc. Alternatively, a search using the suffix _____itis might lead to bronchitis, ileitis, colitis, pancreatitis, etc. *Sci-Mate*™ can also be used in literature current awareness programs as discussed below. The note-taking and retrieval capabilities afforded by *Sci-Mate*™ or comparable systems represent advances in old skills, and these systems will become widely used in the future.

Keeping Up with the Literature

Millions of books and articles are published in scientific fields each year. In chemistry alone, more than 400,000 articles, patents, books, reports, and other related documents were published annually during the late 1970s.[81] How do researchers keep up with even a small segment of their area of research? How do they simultaneously develop broad perspectives of their discipline and related disciplines? Meeting these seemingly opposite objectives will take planning and commitment. The commitment requires about 15 to 20 hours per week for the master's or doctoral student devoted exclusively to thesis or dissertation research. The planning involves an analysis of your literature needs.

Current awareness needs can be divided into:

- professional literature
- general scientific literature
- specialized literature

Professional literature includes information on the activities of members of a discipline and will be found in magazines and newsletters published by scientific societies. The general scientific literature includes journals and books in one's discipline but not necessarily relevant to one's research. Specialized literature includes reports and monographs with direct relevance to one's research. As one progresses through a graduate career the relative commitments to these three types of literature will vary. For example, the general scientific demands of beginning graduate students are large because of the need to pass core courses and to prepare for candidacy examinations. As students progress in their programs, an awareness of specialized literature has to increase to meet developing commitments to thesis or dissertation research. Furthermore, an early naiveté regarding professional affairs will have to be replaced by increasing awareness if one is to be successful in securing a position after graduation.

Now the question may arise, "How do I implement a current awareness program?" This can be done by:

- systematic visits to the library
- reading and using *Current Contents* weekly
- subscribing to a commercial current awareness service
- using a literature storage and retrieval system
- joining journal clubs and professional societies
- attending lectures and professional meetings

Library Visits

Established researchers love the library. They feel at home within its walls. This affection comes from habits that should begin during a graduate career. An hour or two should be set aside each week to visit the library and to browse through newly received journals and books. This habit is reinforced by dedicating the same time slot each week.

Current Contents

The best way to review recent contents of most journals in a field is to scan *Current Contents*. This set of weekly publications from ISI contains compilations of the contents pages of journals in the following areas:

- Agriculture, biology, and environmental sciences
- Arts and humanities
- Clinical practice
- Compu math
- Engineering, technology, and applied sciences
- Life sciences
- Physical, chemical, and earth sciences
- Social and behavioral sciences

Each issue has a subject and author index complete with addresses of authors designated to receive inquiries and reprint requests.

Requesting reprints of articles from authors is an old tradition in science. It is commonly done by sending a postcard to the author with a description of the article desired. ISI's *The Genuine Article* (formerly *Original Article Text Service* or OATS) is also a source of reprints for nearly all journals covered in *Current Contents*.

Commercial Current Awareness Services

A number of current awareness services are available commercially that provide periodic mailings to subscribers. Examples of these services are given in Table 6. Some supply computer printouts of citations from journals on topics dictated by the subscriber, as exemplified by *Ascatopics*® and *ASCA*®. Other services provide selected sections of indexes. Librarians and an advisor should be consulted on subscription to a desirable service. All of the programs require a significant financial commitment which would have to be approved by an advisor or department chairman.

Literature Storage and Retrieval

Students today have to deal with far more information during their graduate career than did students in previous generations. It is important, therefore, to have a system for the storage and retrieval of notes and reprints from journals. Merely alphabetizing materials according to title and storing them in a box or drawer may be adequate for the items necessary for a single report or publication. The use of such a system for

Table 6 Examples of commercially available current awareness services

Service	Description	Address for Inquiries
Automatic Subject Citation Alert® (ASCA) and ASCATOPICS®	Search services providing weekly reports on articles published in a specific field. ASCA allows more narrow focusing for searches.	Institute for Scientific Information, 3501 Market St., Philadelphia, PA 19104
BIOSIS	Search services for *Biological Abstracts*. Free booklets and free courses on how to use computer services. BIOSIS/CA Selects: 23 separate titles, each on very specific subjects, issued bi-weekly, from the current literature.	BIOSIS User Services Department, 2100 Arch St., Philadelphia, PA 19103
Chemical Abstracts	Search services for *Chemical Abstracts*. Mailings of selected sections of *Chemical Abstracts*. *CA Selects*: 133 separate titles each on specific topics, issued bi-weekly, from the current literature.	Chemical Abstracts Service, P.O. Box 3012, Columbus, OH 43210
Excerpta Medica	Search services, on-line and off-line retrieval.	Journals Department, Excerpta Medica, 3131 Princeton Pike, Lawrenceville, NJ 08648
PsycINFO	Computerized search services.	PsycINFO, American Psychological Association, 1200 Seventeenth St., N.W. Washington, DC 20036

storage of all the materials required during a graduate career, however, will lead to hours of frustration when attempting to retrieve information.

A manual storage and retrieval system for notes and reprints was developed in my laboratories several years ago.[117] It requires use of primary and secondary descriptors which are typed or written in the upper-right-hand corner of each reprint or dated set of notes. The primary descriptor is underlined twice; secondary descriptors are underlined once. Separate 3 × 5 index cards are prepared for each descriptor with a complete citation (authors, title, journal name, volume, inclusive pages, and date) on the primary descriptor card and cross-references on the secondary descriptor cards (see Fig. 8). The cards, and reprints and notes, are filed alphabetically in separate filing cabinets. Where there are multiple notes and reprints with the same primary descriptor, these are subfiled in reverse chronological order. The same type of filing system is used with primary and secondary descriptor cards. This filing system is useful, but it is subject to the following difficulties:

1. The number of descriptors chosen must be reasonable, to limit the time necessary to prepare index cards.
2. Changes in descriptors or addition of descriptors is difficult and time consuming.
3. Retrieval is limited to descriptors.
4. Filing is tedious.

Punch card systems[21] for filing information have been available for many years, but they have disadvantages similar to the above-noted method.

An improved system for filing and locating notes and reprints is the *Sci-Mate™ Personal Data Manager* described earlier. Its use obviates the problems noted with the manual system. Additionally, the *Sci-Mate™* system is compatible with on-line computer search systems which allow the searching of large data bases and the construction of files from several sources through use of a microcomputer.[55] Other companies such as Apple have software for personal filing[101] that are adaptable to reprints and notes. Zelnio et al.[139] developed an algorithm for organizing reprint files using a central university computer. None of the latter systems, however, has all the advantages of *Sci-Mate™*.

Journal Clubs

Participation in journal clubs is an enjoyable way of reviewing literature with friends and colleagues. The groups, developed informally, can gather for one-hour meetings every one or two weeks to discuss journal articles. The group should have a discussion leader at each meeting, who is responsible for reviewing the article(s) in depth. Journal club meetings can be scheduled during lunch hour periods and participants can be encouraged to bring a "bag lunch."

A

```
                                          Cocaine
P. I. Jatlow and D. N. Bailey,
"Gas Chromatographic Analysis for
Cocaine in Human Plasma, with Use
of a Nitrogen Detector,"
Clin. Chem., 21, 1918-1921 (1975).
```

B

```
                              Gas Chromatography

 See:   Cocaine; GC Analysis in Human Plasma,
        w̄ N-Detector
```

Figure 8. Primary (A) and secondary (B) descriptor cards (3 × 5 inches) used in manual literature storage and retrieval systems.

Professional Societies

Professionals need societies and associations to promote their welfare and to provide opportunities for continuing education. Prestigious professional societies in relevant disciplines should be identified early in one's graduate career. An advisor may be helpful in choosing one or two organizations that have provisions for student membership (membership fees for students are often one-fifth or less that of regular membership). After joining, regular mailings of newsletters, magazines, or other periodic notices should be received that help improve one's familiarity with an associated profession. The mailings will also provide information of forthcoming scientific meetings.

Lectures and Professional Meetings

Universities are visited frequently by traveling scholars and scientists. Most university departments schedule seminars for visiting scientists during the academic year, and it is wise to select lectures of interest to attend.

Information on departmental seminars is available through campus publications. Most large universities have public news and information bureaus which publish "campus news" periodicals that contain calendars of forthcoming events. If these cannot be obtained directly, an advisor may be willing to share his or her copy. Many advisors also route special lecture notices after their receipt through campus mail.

Advantage should be taken of opportunities to hear noted scientists in fields of interest. The lectures will often be informative and inspiring since many researchers admit to failures and difficulties that they have experienced in their work.

Professional meeting attendance is important for presentation of scientific papers and for making contacts that may be useful when seeking permanent employment. Besides satisfying these needs, professional meetings give life to the literature. Meetings provide opportunities to hear and visit with scientists whose papers have been read. Opportunities may also exist to visit with representatives of instrument manufacturers, publishers, and other information service organizations. These are worthwhile activities, and it is important to discuss with an advisor the possibilities of attending several regional and national meetings during one's graduate career.

Becoming a good researcher is dependent on developing skills for searching, evaluating, and keeping up with the literature. These skills are essential for three of the most important jobs of a researcher: writing, presenting, and publishing papers and dissertations. These topics are discussed in the following three chapters.

Chapter 8

Writing Skills

> "*. . . you should say what you mean,*" *the March Hare went on.*
> "*I do,*" *Alice hastily replied; "at least — at least I mean what I say — that's the same thing, you know.*"
> "*Not the same thing a bit!*" *said the Hatter. "Why you might just as well say that 'I see what I eat' is the same thing as 'I eat what I see'!*"
>
> — LEWIS CARROLL
> *Alice in Wonderland*

Writing spans the sublime to the ridiculous. All researchers must write. It is, therefore, important to develop approaches and styles that ease the task. Success in graduate school and advancement in a professional career depend on one's writing abilities. As noted by Ewing,[44] ". . . managers judge their assistants, subordinates, and consultants at least partly on the basis of their reports, letters and memoranda. The more powerful and responsible a manager is, the more necessary it is that this be done. . . ." Students should begin early in their graduate careers to improve writing skills. Improvement requires an understanding of the elements of good writing, methods for improving writing skills, and tips on writing specific pieces, from memos to book reviews.

Good writing is seen daily in well-edited books and papers. The lucid nature of good writing has intuitive appeal. In contrast, bad writing is evident in some correspondence, reports, and poorly edited publications. Glib criticisms about writing quality, however, are self-defeating. Writing skills should be evaluated against objective criteria.

Elements of Good Writing

Fielden[47] noted that good writing is characterized by four elements:

1. Thought

71

2. Correctness
3. Appropriateness
4. Readability

Thought

Well-written pieces reflect thoughtfulness. Passages are well organized and faithful to the stated purpose of the work. Good writing is accurate. It contains proper hypotheses, assumptions, and conclusions. It
shows a lack of bias and contains believable justifications. Thoughtful
writing reflects the author's enthusiasm and is properly persuasive. The
art of persuasion is most important in correspondence, grants, and
reports.

Correctness

Good writing contains correct grammar, punctuation, and spelling.
These characteristics tend to be targets for criticism of "poor writers," yet
correct writing is more than "mechanics." Correct writing is coherent. It
is marked by proper syntax and good sentence transitions. Correct
writing is neat. It contains judiciously chosen headings and subdivisions.

Appropriateness

Good writing has the right tone. The reader is neither talked down
to nor buried in verbosity or pompousness. In correspondence, appropriate attitudes are reflected and diplomatic approaches are used. Appropriate writing gives the reader a clear idea of needs and desires.

Readability

Good writing is readable. It flows smoothly. It does not require the
rereading of every other sentence. Readable pieces have a lead-off topic
sentence followed by sentences that outline the work. The reader knows
where the material is heading. Early clues are given on how the work will
turn out.

Readable works have clear transitions from paragraph to paragraph.
Summarizing statements appear periodically that help the reader understand prior text. Ideas are logically presented.

Approaches to Good Writing

Several books have recently been published on writing non-fiction, and researchers will find it useful to read at least one of these. Two good choices are the books by Day[30] and Zinsser.[140] Good writing, like all creative activities, develops with practice and a willingness to try new methods.

Most people find that an outline is a good place to start writing efforts. Once an outline has been developed, it is useful to write against a self-imposed deadline. If the introductory section of a paper is started at 9 a.m., see if it can be finished by noon. I find that the "dither" or tension generated by the deadline helps the creative process.

Preparing Notes and Outlines

Different writing efforts require different degrees of planning. Major writing tasks, such as papers and dissertations, call for review of books, papers, research notebooks, and reports. The notebooks should contain notes and conclusions reached at the time of experimentation. Reports written for an advisor or for a granting agency should be prepared to allow direct transfer of sections to manuscripts. This "makes things count double."

Once references and notes have been gathered, an outline should be prepared for the work to be written. Researchers may use topic or sentence outlines, or a combination of both. Some people like to prepare a "very rough draft" which serves as a basis for their outline. Others like to use an annotated outline containing reference notations and topic sentences.

After the outline is complete, consider having it reviewed by an advisor and friends. It is a good idea to develop a "buddy system" for review of writing efforts. Find one or two friends who write well. Make a pact with them to review each other's work. This arrangement can be immensely helpful during a graduate career.

Different approaches should be tried for the preparation of outlines. Remember that there is no right or wrong way. Find the method that works well for you.

Write, Rewrite, and Rewrite

Writing is difficult, but the best way to start is to start. Some words on paper "fuel" further efforts. Follow an outline. Try beginning with a topic sentence, and follow with some sentences that outline the paragraphs to come. The actual act of writing will help the creative process. Use lined paper when writing by hand. As words are put on paper or appear on a computer screen, new ideas will emerge.

Write simply. Stick to short subject-verb-object sentences. Avoid long beginning adjectival phrases that the reader is forced to remember before coming to the subject of the sentence.

Keep sentences under 40 words. Produce contiguous sentences of varying lengths. Include summary sentences at the end of major sections. Once the writing has begun, try to get as much as possible on paper without stopping. Worry about revision later.

Try using an outline as a To Do List. As sections are completed, check them off. After completing an emotionally exhausting section, reward yourself with a fresh cup of coffee or a walk around the room. This allows time to reflect on accomplishments and to encourage subsequent efforts. Use headings liberally. One accepted format is:

MAIN HEADING

Main Subheading
   Text begins here . . .

   Secondary subheading. Text begins here . . .

Use the active voice rather than the passive voice where possible. Try not to impress rather than inform. Americans have a tendency to try to sound important. Our main faults are verbosity and excessive use of jargon. These failings also lead to problems with syntax.

Jargon includes confused, strange, technical, obscure, and often pretentious language. Technical words must be used in scientific writing, but they should be properly defined. All other forms of jargon should be avoided. Examples of jargon and preferred alternatives are given in Appendix 2.

With practice, writing styles can be improved. Booth[16] suggests writing as though you were talking to the reader. The "talk" must be grammatically correct and devoid of colloquialisms. This approach is aided by consciously trying to speak well. The training includes speaking slowly, choosing words deliberately, and finishing each sentence. Approaches to writing styles are described by Zinsser[140] and Strunk and White.[123] Other style manuals have been reviewed by Stainton.[119]

Revision is an indispensable part of writing. Good authors revise their works five or more times. The revision process provides the best opportunity to clarify thoughts and to correct possible contradictions. Try to develop empathy for the reader. Keep asking, "Could I understand this material if I were reading it for the first time?" Try thinking of how the work would appear to a reader whose native tongue is not English.

During the revision process, try to cut out wordiness. The clutter is minimized by eliminating adjectives and adverbs as much as possible. We overuse words such as: very, quite, rather, fairly, relatively, several, and much. In English, nouns may be used to modify nouns. These noun adjectives (e.g., gas engine, monoamine oxidase, life science) are useful, but can become confusing if stacked (e.g., albino mouse liver monoamine oxidase).

There are different approaches to the revision process. Tichy[128] recommends "cooling" or allowing a piece to sit for a day or longer before revision. Some writers wait a week. This helps to see work as others will see it. It is often surprising how confusing complex sentences or phrases seem after they have "cooled off" for a few days.

A second revision process, recommended by Mullins,[90] calls for section rewriting.

1. Write first section and leave it alone.
2. Revise first section before writing second section.
3. Revise first and second sections before writing third section.
4. Etc.

The Mullins method works best if a work is completed in six sections or less. Otherwise, unnecessary repetition is introduced before the last section is written.

A third method for revision involves reading passages aloud. This helps uncover awkward and confusing sentences. Regardless of the method used, the revision process should be done slowly and repeatedly until you are satisfied. The task is simplified by a cut-and-paste method or by use of a word processor. The final revised work should be reviewed by an advisor and writing "buddies." Ask for a tough review, and respond constructively.

Writing Tools

The tools of a good writer include: dictionaries, synonym finders, specialized handbooks, and grammar and composition guides. *Webster's Third New International Dictionary,*[134] *Webster's New Collegiate Dictionary,*[133] and the *Random House Dictionary*[105] have been recommended for scientists. A *Roget's Thesaurus*[110] or its equivalent, *The Synonym Finder,*[125] are invaluable. It is also useful to have a personal copy of a science dictionary such as the *Dictionary of Science & Technology,*[35] the *Longman Dictionary of Scientific Usage,*[56] or the well-illustrated *Dictionary of Scientific and Technical Terms.*[36] Specialized dictionaries for engineering, medical, and physical scientists have been catalogued by Stainton.[120] The *Van Nostrand Scientific Encyclopedia,*[130] for example, contains a wealth of information in a single volume.

A guide to English usage and grammar should be obtained. Several of these are available, such as the works by Partridge[97] and by Perrin and Smith.[100] The question may now arise, "How will I afford all these books?" The purchase of an English dictionary, synonym finder, and scientific dictionary should be a student's responsibility. Other references may be available in the laboratory or study area for graduate students in an advisor's group. Research grants provide funds for the purchase of books. If the reference books cited are not available, an advisor may be persuaded to buy some with his or her grant money. University libraries will also have the reference works cited.

Notes, Memoranda, and Letters

Written communications include notes, memoranda and letters. I differentiate between notes and memoranda. Notes are short informal messages to friends and acquaintances. Memoranda are more formal than notes, and they are reserved for correspondence between persons within the university. Letters are the most formal type of correspondence.

Written communications should be used when necessary, but the overuse of notes and memoranda should be avoided. The time needed to communicate orally should be balanced against the time needed for writing. Written communications should be used only when they save time or when it is necessary to document events.

Notes should be dated and contain the full name of the recipient. Here is an example of a format for notes:

Joseph Procter
03-19-83

Joe,

Your books are ready at the printer.

Bob

Memoranda can be written using this format:

TO:
FROM:
RE:

The "RE" informs the recipient about the subject of the memorandum. The body of the memo is developed using the communicator's guide:

- Here's where I am . . .
- Here's how I got there . . .
- Here's what I want from you . . .

Below is an example of a properly constructed memorandum from the chairman of a human subjects institutional review board to a graduate student researcher.

March 14, 1983

TO: Mary Markley,
          Department of Psychology

FROM: Albert B. Prescott, Chairman, IRB

RE: IRB Meeting, March 28, 1983

You are invited to attend the IRB meeting scheduled for Monday, March 28, 1983, at 4:00 p.m. in the Main Building, Room 6.204.

Our IRB regularly meets with investigators whose proposals are being considered for approval. We hope that you can be present at our meeting to answer questions about your proposal, "Alienation in Sensory Deprived Patients." Thank you for your cooperation.

This memo is direct, yet courteous. It fulfills the goals of the communicator's guide and gives enough information for the recipient to respond correctly.

The format for business letters is:

Your address
Date

Title, name, position
and address of recipient

Re: (optional)

Salutation: (or ,)

Body of Letter.

Complimentary close,

Your signature

Your name typed
and your position

Enclosures: (list them)

Your initials in capital letters followed by / or :, then the initials of the typist in lower case letters

The recipient should be addressed properly. If he or she has an earned doctorate, Dr. (or Doctor) can be used or the initials of the highest earned degree can be placed after the recipient's name (e.g., Joseph E. Sinsheimer, Ph.D.; Elaine S. Waller, Pharm. D.). Faculty may be addressed as professor if appropriate. It is better to address non-doctoral professorial faculty as Professor than Mr. Be sensitive to national customs and individual preferences. In some countries (e.g., Federal Republic of Germany, Switzerland) it is common to refer to doctoral faculty as Dr. Prof. or Herr Dr. Prof. Some women prefer Mrs. or Miss to Ms., and they will indicate this in their correspondence. Retired deans and professors may be correctly referred to as Dean and Professor, respectively.

The titles of the recipients' positions should be added after their names (e.g., Howard B. Lassman, Ph.D., Director of Clinical Pharmacology; Mary H. Ferguson, Ph.D., Editor). This is proper protocol for all professional administrators. The remainder of the address should be complete and it may contain accepted abbreviations (e.g., Company, Co.; Incorporated, Inc.).

The "Re" is useful in citing important numerical notations. Manuscripts considered for publication have number assignments that should be referred to in correspondence containing revisions. Letters referring to orders for merchandise should include purchase order numbers (e.g., Re: Order no. 27,632A).

The salutation should read Dear Dr. (Prof., Mr., Ms., etc.) followed by a colon. A colon is proper when the recipient is not known well. First names followed by a comma can be used for friends. When no specific person is addressed Dear Sir/Madam can be used. Other salutations include Dear Person or Dear People, or Dear, followed by a word denoting the person's profession. A letter to a pharmacist, for example, might include the salutation, Dear Pharmacist (surname):. Analogous salutations can be constructed for accountants, architects, dentists, engineers, nurses, etc. This approach helps avoid allegations of sexism.

The body of the letter is developed by using the communicator's guide. Letters are longer than memos but should be restricted to one page if possible. Necessary details can be included in appendices that should be properly labeled to prevent loss.

The tone of letters should vary according to their purpose (see Table 7). Most Americans welcome informality. Other nationalities tend to be more formal. Try to strike a balance between stuffiness which is unbecoming and casualness which may be insulting.

The complimentary close may read Yours truly, Yours faithfully, or Yours sincerely. Some prefer a simple Sincerely.

Persuasiveness

Memos, letters, and prospective portions of reports and grants may require persuasion. There are strategies for being persuasive. Understand that the persuasion referred to is not that of the huckster. Assertions must be based on facts. Arguments should be developed logically. Sensational

Table 7 Different types of letters and their tone[a]

Purpose of Letter	Tone
Request for details (of an appointment, a research grant, an item of equipment). Invitation to a speaker.	Clear, simple, direct, and courteous.
Application for an appointment or a grant. Includes evidence of suitability and is usually supported by additional information on separate sheets (e.g., details of applicant and proposed research project).	Clear, direct, and factual. Confident but not aggressive.
Complaint	Clear and direct but not aggressive.
Reply (to an inquiry or complaint) giving information, instruction or, explanation. Reply to all the points raised in the inquiry.	Clear, direct, informative, polite, helpful and sincere.
Acknowledgment of an inquiry or application	Simple and direct.
Letter of thanks	Appreciative.

[a] From R. Barrass, Scientists must write, p. 18, Chapman and Hall, London, 1978. Reprinted by permission of the publisher.

claims or examples should be avoided. Ewing[44] suggested that, if you have a sympathetic reader, arguments can be ordered with the strongest appearing last. Lead off with the strongest argument if the reader is unsympathetic.

Try appealing to positions held by the individual or institution. A university or industrial firm committed to excellence in research will be affected positively by arguments for policy changes that elevate standards.

Copies of memos or letters can be used to one's benefit. An extra copy judiciously sent (i.e., as indicated by an "xc" and the recipient's name in the lower left-hand corner of the letter) to an official higher than the recipient can provide a useful power play.

Be cautious with power plays. They should be used only as a last resort. A complaint to a professor about her or his performance in a course, written with an xc to the department chairman, can backfire. Misunderstanding of a situation could create ill feelings and cause repercussions later. Honest dialogue is better than confrontation.

Students sometimes harbor a fantasy that begins with their righteous correction of a professor's errors during a seminar or lecture. This act is met by thunderous applause and a humbling of the professor. A reverse approach, however, is often more effective. Confidential memos or letters call for honest dialogue. If this doesn't work, the xc tactic can be used.

Research Notebooks

The research notebook is used to prepare a record of experimental work. It is also a repository for diagrams, graphs, and standardization routines that permit repetition of experiments. A research notebook should be bound with stiff covers and may have loose-leaf pages. Its pages should be consecutively numbered, and the book should contain a table of contents, preferably at the beginning.

Copies of all notebook entries should be prepared and stored in a safe place. Loss of notes through fire or other accidents can be catastrophic.

Notebook descriptions of experiments should include:

1. Title, date, and purpose
2. List of required equipment and materials
3. Outline of procedures
4. Observations and data
5. Graphical representations of data
6. Equations, calculations, and statistical tests
7. Records of unusual events that may influence results
8. Conclusions
9. Modified hypotheses and plans for future experiments
10. Researcher's signature

If an experiment resembles a previous one, page references may be substituted for items 2 and 3. Data can be collected on data sheets specifically designed for the experiment. All data sheets should contain units of measurement in column headings. Times of data collection should also be noted on the data sheets. The sheets should be affixed to notebook pages when experiments are complete. Avoid recording data on loose scraps of paper that can be lost. Sections of the notebook should not be rewritten because errors can be made during transcription of data.

Notebook entries end with conclusions and descriptions of unusual events that may have influenced the results. Conclusions should be analyzed in terms of experimental hypotheses. If necessary, alternative hypotheses and experiments should be proposed. Completed notebook entries should be signed and the signature of a witness added if plans exist to apply for a patent.

The research notebook is an important part of research. It is not, however, useful in conveying results to others. This activity requires a report.

Reports

Report writing is an integral part of research. Paradis[96] notes that the preparation of reports and related pieces (e.g., research articles) requires as much as one-third of the time of professionals who choose a career in research. If a career is chosen in a highly regulated industry (e.g., pharmaceuticals) or in government, the requirement for report writing will increase.

Reports should answer the following questions:

- What are you trying to do?
- Do the methods and conclusions make sense?
- What is the importance of the work?

Report writing skills are beneficial throughout a graduate career. The practice gained in writing reports will also help in the preparation of research articles, grant proposals, and the dissertation. The importance of report writing makes it imperative that a research advisor be chosen who regularly requires this activity. A good advisor will also prepare timely critiques of work. This forces students to gain the necessary writing experience.

Report writing helps to clarify one's thoughts about research. John Stuart Mill[87] once noted, "Hardly any original thoughts on mental or social subjects ever make their way among mankind, or assume their proper importance in the minds even of their inventors, until aptly selected words or phrases have, as it were, nailed them down and held them fast." Reports are useful at three stages of research: at the beginning, during difficulties, and at project's end. During the development of a research project the report should include:

1. A statement of the problem and underlying hypotheses
2. Analysis of how the problem developed
3. Description of possible solutions
4. Steps to be used to implement preferred solutions
5. Costs

Intervening reports help researchers confront anomalies in data, plan new experiments, and modify hypotheses. As noted by Beveridge,[10] "The systematic arrangement of the data often discloses flaws in the reasoning, or alternative lines of thought which had been missed. Assumptions and conclusions at first accepted as 'obvious' may even prove indefensible when set down clearly and examined critically." Final reports serve as preludes to manuscripts for publication.

Report Format and Style

Here is a good format for interim and final research reports:

- Title
- Table of Contents
- Abstract
- Introduction
- Experimental Section
- Results
- Discussion
- Bibliography
- Appendices

The title page contains the full title and name of the author(s), department, and university. Titles should indicate the subject and scope of the report. Avoid unnecessary words in the title such as: Investigations of . . . , Interesting Aspects of . . . , and Results of. . . . Develop a title that is a label rather than a sentence. Use noun adjectives and correct syntax. Do not use abbreviations, chemical formulas, proprietary names, or jargon in a title. Ask these questions about the title: How will it look as a title to a paper? Does it entice the reader into the rest of the report?

The title page should bear the date of the report, and a serial number if this is the practice in your department. Do not number the title page. Its imaginary number is "i" if the report has a table of contents. If the report is short and contains no table of contents, then the title page bears an imaginary "1."

A table of contents is useful for reports longer than 10 pages. It can be composed of headings and subheadings from the body of the report and their corresponding page numbers. Subheadings are indented from headings and may be used selectively. Try to keep the length of the table of contents to one page. If it is longer, use the numbering *ii, iii, iv,* etc. for continuation pages. The table of contents and subsequent sections are numbered at the lower center of each page.

The abstract is the most important part of a report. It is the section read by most people, and it gives readers an overview of the report. The abstract, therefore, should be written last and with special care. Here are the sections of the abstract and sources of material for each:

- Statement of the problem — Introduction
- Brief description of methodology — Materials and Methods
- Main findings — Results
- Conclusions — Discussion

The abstract should be written simply. Use the past tense, write in the third person, and minimize the use of technical language. Include only ideas and claims found in the report. The abstract of a report describing a new method should contain the method's basic principles, range of operation, and degrees of accuracy and precision.

Abstracts should not include references to tables and figures, descriptions of published work, or reference citations. Conclude the abstract with one or two major points from the discussion.

The introduction of a report should be written first. Begin the introduction with a statement of the problem. Continue with background information, and add reference citations using the Harvard system (see below). Previous work should be surveyed, but not in an encyclopedic way. It is not necessary to cite every known reference. The introduction should contain a review of the material presented in the report. This helps the reader decide whether it is worth continuing. Introductions should be interesting and should inspire further reading.

The experimental section contains descriptions of experiments and methods. Include enough details to permit repetition of the experiments, but omit procedures already reported. Develop the experimental section in a sensible order. Don't be afraid to deviate from the chronology of the experimental work. A research report should not read like a diary. Rather, experiments should be arranged logically to benefit the reader.

Use headings to highlight paragraphs describing materials, equipment, methods, and experiments. The materials and equipment listings should include sources and manufacturers, respectively. Give technical specifications and purities of reference chemicals and materials. Provide accurate identifications of animals, plants, and microorganisms, including genera, species, and strains. Animals should also be described by weight, age, sex, and special handling. Experimental sections for human subjects research should include selection criteria and details of informed consent procedures.

Descriptions of methods and experiments should contain the *what*, *where*, *when*, and *how* of procedures. Use abbreviations and a format approved by the journal that will publish the work. Do not repeat published procedures, but do cite germane references. If the published method is complex, give a two- or three-sentence description of it, using an introduction such as, "The method of Frank (10) was used. Briefly, it involved . . . ." This helps the reader develop a conceptual understanding of the results without having to consult another paper.

The results section should be written after the introduction and experimental sections. Describe the results in the past tense using the chronology established in the two previous sections. Do not repeat material from the experimental section. The experimental section is a description of *what was done*. The results section helps to describe *what happened*.

Tables should be prepared to stand alone. The reader should be able to make sense of a table without reading the entire report. This is accomplished through clear titles and headings, and well-developed footnotes. Column headings can be abbreviated and should contain units of measurements. Columns containing descriptive material and independent variables should appear on the left. Columns for dependent variables go on the right. Table 8 is an example of a well-constructed table. Note how like elements are read down. Compare the format of Table 8 with that of Table 9. The cross listing of the like elements in Table 9 makes it more difficult to comprehend. Number tables consecutively, and refer to them in numerical order in the results section.

Day[30] refers to graphs as pictorial tables. Tables help with the listing of data, and graphs help depict trends in data. Graphs are useful in planning experiments and should be used liberally in reports prepared for an advisor. Use copies of graphs made directly from those in your research notebook. Make sure, however, that all ordinates and abscissas are properly labeled. The ordinate and abscissa points should not extend beyond the plotted data points. Graphs containing several lines should have different symbols for each. The following set is recommended for use with solid or dashed lines: ○ ● △ ▲ □ ■. Use the filled-in symbols to draw the reader's attention to a line that is emphasized in the text. Special

Table 8   Characteristics of fruit-bearing plants of North America[a]

Plant	Avg. Growing Season (mo)[b]	Avg. Height (cm)[c]	Color of Fruit	Avg. Yield of Fruit (kg/plant)[c]
Grapefruit	4.2	400	Yellow	170
Lemon	5.6	300	Yellow	30.0
Lime	5.2	275	Green	25.5
Strawberry	8.0	5.75	Red	0.090
Tomato	9.2	180	Red	5.00

[a] Bogus data.

[b] In South Texas.

[c] During growing season.

Table 9 Characteristics of fruit-bearing plants of North America[a]

Determination	Grapefruit	Lemon	Lime	Strawberry	Tomato
Avg. growing season (mo)[a]	4.2	5.6	5.2	8.0	9.2
Avg. height (cm)[b]	400	300	275	5.75	180
Color of fruit	Yellow	Yellow	Green	Red	Red
Avg. yield of fruit (kg/plant)[c]	170	30.0	25.5	0.090	5.00

[a] Bogus data.
[b] In South Texas.
[c] During growing season.

care must be taken if graphs are being prepared for reports that will go outside of your advisor's research group. These graphs should be constructed using guidelines given under "Research Papers."

The discussion is written after the results. It should not, however, recapitulate the results. Continue to write in the active voice when appropriate. Put the results in context with published work. Use the past tense when referring to your results and the present tense for published results. Until work has been subjected to peer review and published, it should be considered tentative. In contrast, published work is accepted. Avoid anthropomorphic expressions such as: The results suggest . . . , The instrument measured . . . , and The data point to . . . Results, instruments, and data are capable of such feats only in cartoons.

Discuss the theoretical and practical importance of the work, and include the possible implications of failures experienced. Remember that you cannot prove negatives. As noted by Sagan,[113] ". . . absence of evidence is not evidence of absence." Confront ambiguities and apparent contradictions in the work. When choosing between hypotheses, remember Occam's razor—the scientist prefers the simplest explanation that agrees with all the evidence. Be careful not to introduce observations into the discussion that were not covered in the results. Limit speculations; assess the importance of the findings on the basis of previously published work.

The discussion section should be completed with plans for the near future (i.e., 2 to 6 weeks). Give a brief description of what experiments will be done, and indicate what the results of these experiments are expected to be. Suggest how these results might affect current hypotheses. Indicate any problems or special needs that can be anticipated during the planned experiments.

The bibliography should be prepared in the format of the journal that may publish the work. Journals use three bibliographic systems:

- Harvard system
- Citation order
- Alphabet–number system

The Harvard system involves the use of a surname notation for citing references in the text. The reports of Hurley (1976) and Hurley and Thurston (1982) are referred to with names and dates (in parentheses) as indicated, or as follows: "Anthramycin antitumor agents have been evaluated (Hurley, 1976; Hurley and Thurston, 1982) in . . ." Citations with three authors appear as Hurley, Thurston, and Kaplan (1983) the first time they are cited and as Hurley et al. (1983) or (Hurley et al., 1983) subsequently. The last two formats are used uniformly for references having four or more authors. When there are two or more "Hurley (1976)" references, the first one cited becomes Hurley (1976a) and the second becomes Hurley (1976b). The reference list is compiled alphabetically for the bibliography. References such as Hurley, 1976a, Hurley, 1976b, Hurley, 1977, and Hurley, 1978 are arranged chronologically and alphabetically.

The Harvard system helps during writing and revision. Citations can be noted in the developing text without stopping to write out the reference. The name citations are used later to prepare note cards each bearing a single complete reference. References can easily be added or deleted from the alphabetized note cards. Similar routines can be developed with word processors.

The citation order system uses a series of numbers starting with "1" to identify references. Number assignments follow the order of appearance of references in the report. The bibliography lists the references in numerical order.

The alphabet–number system is similar to the Harvard system, which is often used during the writing process and in compiling the reference list. Subsequent use of the alphabet–number system requires numbering of the alphabetized reference list. The numbers are then substituted for the author–date entries in the report. Numbers are used parenthetically or as superscripts depending on the format of the journal that may publish the work.

The references in a report should be checked against the original literature. Make sure that each reference is accurately cited. Do the references contain the material claimed? Are the names, dates, and volume and page numbers correct? This is a tedious process, but references "locked into" a report will result in time savings during subsequent writing efforts.

A common system of abbreviations has been developed by the American National Standards Institute[4] for journal title words, as indicated by Day.[30] These should be used uniformly except for one-word journal titles (e.g., *Science, Psychopharmacology*), which are unabbreviated. Abbreviations of words like arachnology (spiders), entomology (insects), and ichthyology (fish) always end after the . . . ol. The standard abbreviations are used with the volume–page number–year format of the journal you intend to publish in.

Quotations require special care. All words and punctuation marks must be checked to assure that they are correct. Partial quotes ". . . are denoted with three dots" as indicated. Check for proper placement and use of diacritical marks (such as the two dots of the umlaut) in foreign words.

Appendices containing supplementary data may be added after the bibliography. Number them sequentially and use title and column headings similar to those in tables. Detailed instructions for routine analyses (federal officials are fond of calling these standard operating procedures or SOPs) can be included as appendices to monthly research reports. Copies of these can be posted in the laboratory for daily use. Write-ups for computer routines, animal care procedures, and screening protocols for human subjects research are also good appendix materials. There should be a feeling of pride when your first research report is completed. Later, the value of reports will be realized during the development of research papers and your dissertation.

Research Papers

There are several types of research papers. The four most common are:

- Articles or full-length papers
- Notes
- Communications
- Letters

Articles are written to describe extensive and definitive studies. The format and style of articles are similar to those in research reports. The elements of research reports are listed in Table 10 along with modifications that are necessary to prepare articles. The recommendations are general and given as guidance. Before preparing any research paper, check the "instructions to authors" found periodically in issues of journals. The text material for research papers is often distilled from several research reports, and a cut-and-paste method or a word processor will help you prepare composite material.

Footnotes can support statements that do not fit easily into the results and discussion. Some journals require the use of footnotes for

Table 10   Recommendations for converting research reports
into research articles

Format Element of Research Report	Changes Needed to Prepare Research Article
Title Page	Add key words for literature retrieval system.[a]
Abstract	Statements may require numbering depending on journal.
Table of Contents	Omit.
Experimental	You may use tables to list large numbers of research specimens (e.g., plants, animals).
Results	Avoid presentation of negative results.
Discussion	Limit speculation, discussion of negative results, and plans for future research.
—	Add summary and conclusion sections as required by journal.
—	Add acknowledgment section to express gratitude to: funding sources[b] and faculty, students, or staff.
Bibliography	Note system used by journal.
Appendices	Omit.

[a] Check journal instructions for relevance and limitations.
[b] Include grant numbers when relevant.

proprietary and manufacturers' names. Footnotes can also be used to respond to criticisms of reviewers, but they should not be overused. Twedt[129] refers to the overuse as "footnoteitis." Symptoms of "footnoteitis" are observed when half or more of the text manuscript pages is devoted to footnotes.

Tables and graphs require special attention when papers are prepared for publication. The number of tables and graphs should be limited. Find ways of incorporating mean data into the text. If tables are needed, use the guidelines described under research reports.

Graphs are known as line drawings to printers, and they must be prepared carefully to permit effective reproduction. The suggestion made earlier about lifting graphs from research notebooks is unacceptable for research papers. Graphs have to be drawn with black ink on plain white paper or on paper with light-blue grid marks. Limit the number of curves on a graph to six, and use alternating open and filled symbols as noted earlier. Make sure the letters of the ordinate and abscissa labels are large enough to allow for photoreduction. Never try to label graphs with a typewriter. Typed letters and numbers are rarely large or dark enough. Use alternate numbering of stub-lines of graphs. This permits the use of larger numbers.

Photos (with dimensions recommended by the journal) of graphs should be prepared and submitted for publication rather than original drawings. Write your name lightly in pencil on the back of each photograph, making sure the imprint does not show on the front of the photograph. Save the original drawings to prepare slides for presentations.

Figure legends are usually typed on separate pages. Include enough information in the legend to permit the figure to stand alone. A key for different curves [e.g., shear-stress as a function of temperature: carbon steel (O), vanadium steel (●), and iron (△)] must be included.

Black and white photographs or micrographs can be used for figures. Alternatively, color photographs can be used but the resulting images are not distinct. The cost of this so-called halftone work may be 100 dollars or more, and this cost is often passed on to the authors. Reproductions of color photos can cost thousands of dollars. In some research, however, a picture is worth a thousand words and the cost of photographic illustrations is justified.

Expert help should be obtained in preparing clear photographs. If the subject matter is a set of small objects (e.g., micrographs of colonies of microorganisms), crop the photograph to accentuate the set. Arrows, numbers, or letters can be placed at key points on the photograph. This is done with press-on letters, numbers, and symbols including arrows such as the ones available through the Datak Corp., Guttenberg, N.J. Be sure to identify the additions in the figure legend. Write your name or all the authors' surnames lightly in pencil on the back of each photograph and micrograph. Also with pencil, mark the top of each photograph with an arrow.

Watch the numbering of tables and figures. Many journals use Roman numerals for tables and Arabic numbers for figures. Find out if the word "Figure" can be abbreviated in the text and figure legends. Write in the words table and figure with appropriate numbers in the margins at points in the text where the tables and figures should appear in the published paper. Use blue pencil if the paper is to be directly photo-reproduced.

Notes, communications, and letters have different purposes and styles than research articles. Notes are used to describe definitive, though shorter, studies than those presented in articles. Some journals dispense with the abstract in notes; otherwise, the format of notes is the same as that of articles.

Communications and letters are short (i.e., less than five typewritten pages) papers of unusual importance. Manuscripts prepared as communications are rarely divided into formal sections. Rather, the text contains elements from the introduction, experimental, results, and discussion sections. The brevity of communications and letters requires a minimum of figures and tables. The figures and tables that are included, however, must be accompanied by experimental detail. Examples of well-prepared figures and tables can be found in most issues of *Science* and *Nature*.

Research papers should be typed according to the instructions to authors of the journal of choice. This typically involves double-spaced typing on bond paper with 2.5- to 3.5-centimeter margins. Number each page in the upper right-hand corner starting with page two.

Book Reviews

It may be rare for graduate students in some disciplines to prepare book reviews for publication. Book reviews, however, are commonly prepared by graduate professionals. Thus, it is helpful to gain the necessary experience during an academic career, perhaps through joint reviews with an advisor — an activity that would be appropriate for this book.

Book reviews are solicited by journal editors who supply a gratis copy of the book for the review. The following evaluations will be expected:

- The range and nature of the book
- Whether or not the book meets the author's stated purpose
- How the book fits into a field or discipline
- The appropriateness of the references cited
- How the book compares with other published works
- The themes or theses developed by the author
- Typographical and grammatical errors
- The style and accuracy of the text

Keep the criticisms objective and constructive. Avoid personal attacks even if you know and dislike the author. Remember that scholars and their work will be remembered long after the work of critics.

Briefly review the background and credentials of the author. This is most important in the social sciences. Hammett noted[60] that the approaches of scholars such as historians and sociologists are often influenced by the personal situation of the author.

Watch the length requirement established by the journal for the review. Follow format guidelines carefully, and supply necessary ancillary information such as biographical data on the author(s).

Few graduate students write books during their academic careers. For this reason, it can be difficult for them to develop the empathy necessary to review others' books. Once students have begun writing their theses or dissertations, however, they begin to understand the rigors of producing book-length works. Guidelines for preparing theses and dissertation are contained in the next chapter.

Chapter 9

Preparing Theses and Dissertations

. . . nearly all the successful writers I have
known had to make the dissertation close
to an obsession. . . .
— DAVID STERNBERG

Most master's degree and all Ph.D. degree programs require original contributions to research that are documented in a thesis or dissertation. The thesis or dissertation requirement can be anticipated with anxiety, or steps can be taken to prepare for it and ease the task. Several books[20,80,122,124] have been written that include guidelines for the preparation of dissertations. In this chapter I will review suggestions made by the authors of these works. I will also propose approaches and methods that can be instituted early in a graduate career to lessen the difficulty of meeting the dissertation requirement.

Planning and Approaches

The ways in which dissertations have been written are probably as numerous as the resulting documents; however, three general approaches are prevalent:

1. Begin writing when all research is complete.
2. Combine two or more major research papers.
3. Develop several writing projects throughout the graduate career that become the basis for the dissertation.

The first method includes preparation of a dissertation proposal and research summaries, but the major writing task is left to the last few months of graduate work. This is commonplace in many laboratory-based sciences. In the social–behavorial sciences, the writing–research efforts are often intermingled over a period of one to two years. For the laboratory researcher, the late preparation method is a source of frustration, and of an almost overwhelming fear of the "final writing task." Delays occur because of inadequate analysis and summarization of research results during the course of the work. The fear of writing escalates as the research notebooks get thicker and more numerous. Obviously, the late preparation method is not recommended.

A second method of dissertation preparation involves the joining of two or more full-length research papers through appropriate introductory and transition sections. This method has become more popular in laboratory-based sciences in recent years. It requires the development of definitive research papers, but it results in a somewhat less cohesive end product. For one thing, journal editors will not allow the publication of extensive historical reviews and the many figures that generally appear in dissertations. Use of the research paper composite method may also be opposed by tradition-bound faculty.

The third approach to dissertation preparation is one I refer to as the hierarchical method. This method requires planning and coordination of writing activities throughout one's graduate program.

Doctoral students encounter the following writing assignments during their graduate careers:

1. Dissertation and grant proposals
2. Research reports
3. Term papers for courses
4. Research papers
5. Written candidacy reports or proposals
6. Dissertation

The hierarchical system requires the dovetailing of purposes and objectives of as many of the above assignments as possible. Early planning is essential for use of this system.

If you adopt the hierarchical system, discuss it with an advisor as soon as possible. Determine whether departmental or program rules forbid orienting the writing projects as proposed. In some programs, for example, students may not develop a candidacy proposal akin to their doctoral research.

Instructors usually permit a choice of term paper topics in elective courses so long as the topics are relevant to course objectives. Why not choose topics that will have to be covered in the dissertation historical review? Additionally, instructors of research methods or scientific writing courses may permit preparation of the introduction of a thesis as a course requirement. The dovetailing of course and dissertation objectives is a good way of making things count double.

Dissertation writing is also eased by a focused approach to experimental work. Experienced researchers relate how they mentally plan tables and figures when designing and conducting experiments. This type of focusing helps to keep the final dissertation effort uppermost in one's mind, which encourages efficiency.

Use of the hierarchical method should promote close contact with an advisor. Joint planning efforts will include intermingling of purposes of writing papers, careful review of intervening writing efforts (e.g., research papers), and a sharing of perceptions of how much work will be necessary to complete the dissertation research.

Characteristics of Theses and Dissertations

The graduate thesis or dissertation is generally encyclopedic in nature. It contains an extensive survey of the literature, including historical background. The model dissertation is highly illustrated with diagrams, photographs, and charts. Tables and examples abound, providing broad perspectives on the dissertation subject. A prize-winning dissertation at the University of Texas at Austin (*Dynamics of Huastec Ethnobotany: Resources, Resource Perception and Resource Management*) in 1983 exemplifies the model dissertation. The work was completed by Janice B. Alcorn, who lived for more than a year with the Huastec Indians, studying their culture and learning their language. Alcorn's findings included maps of vegetative zones, diagrams of houses and farmsteads, and line drawings of local ethnogeography. The dissertation narrative contained a comprehensive analysis of the ecology, culture, and sociology of Huastec life. A work of immense proportion was produced. Similar models of excellence should be sought by all writers of theses and dissertations.

Dissertation Blues

Negative feelings that occur during the research and writing stages of dissertations[122] can be described as dissertation blues. Heading the list of dissertation blues is the sense of being overwhelmed. This feeling is most prevalent when plans for the dissertation are not developed early in one's program.

Feelings that the wrong project was chosen plague graduate researchers, especially when results do not develop as expected. Commitment and self-assurance are necessary to plod ahead. Encouragement can be found in the work of others. John Sheehan, the first chemist to synthesize penicillin, reflected[115] on the dark days leading up to his success:

No matter how discouraging the laboratory work turned out to be, I simply went back in and tried more approaches. I went back to the library and read more research reports. I thought more about the problem. As long as I could avoid asking myself the defeating question "Should I really be in this?", I remained immune to the anxieties that accompany scientific research. For me it was always forward march, never halt, never retreat.

Commitment like that of Sheehan is aided by publication of intermediary results, as noted with the hierarchical system.

Dissertation researchers often have nightmares about their hypotheses being wrong or their experiments leaving something out. Such worries are frequently alleviated by conducting good control experiments. The control experiments may be suggested during the course of experimentation or after experiments have been conducted. Patience and perseverance are necessary to follow through with the control experiments, and to correct results accordingly.

Writer's block or the apparent inability to put thoughts to paper is a common myth about dissertation writers. As indicated in Chapters 4 and 8, writers need schedules and determination to write around or through "writer's block."

Worries about being scooped are common among dissertation researchers. These concerns come from the notion that the whole dissertation project will have to be abandoned if a similar paper appears in print before completion of the research work. A related fear is that published work was not picked up in the literature search before the dissertation project was begun. This latter problem is addressed by searches through overlapping data bases, and the review of bibliographic entries in current publications. Most often, earlier thoroughness is confirmed. The occurrence of simultaneous publications is common in science, and it results from different groups working at the forefront of science. Consolation is derived from the idea that the literature serves to inform and confirm results. Furthermore, it would be rare if two researchers approached a problem with identical methodology. Thus, completed research should be publishable even if similar results have unbeknowingly been obtained elsewhere.

Dissertation blues also include a feeling of becoming "burned out." Extended and concentrated efforts create the illusion of losing track of the world and becoming mentally exhausted. For scholars this is parallel to the training of long-distance runners. The dissertation work serves as a prelude to long-term projects that are essential during all professional careers. Just as the runner needs weeks or months to build endurance, the scholar builds perseverance and feelings of self-worth through the rigors of the dissertation process.

Relations with Dissertation Committee Members

Dissertation committees operate differently in various universities. Sometimes, graduate students have close relationships with their committees. Alternatively, students may interact with their committees only during the final stages of the dissertation research.

The policy on dissertation committees should be determined early in a graduate career. An active and helpful committee is desirable, as indicated in Chapter 3. In some cases, it is wise to petition for a co-advisor if the expertise of a committee member is found to be crucial to the dissertation research.

Students should be sensitive to expectations of the committee. Interim abstracts and reports should be developed according to a schedule prepared with an advisor. All outlines, abstracts, reports, and dissertation sections should be reviewed by an advisor before being distributed to committee members.

Approaches to Writing

Guidelines for the preparation of a thesis or dissertation are similar to those described in Chapters 4 and 8 for preparing research papers. The major difference between writing a research paper and writing a dissertation is the length of time necessary for the latter effort. Consequently, it is wise to find a suitable space for dissertation writing. The "space" should preferably be near the library. It should be secure enough that books and papers can be left from day-to-day, and it should preferably be off-limits to family and friends. Try to obtain a "space" with characteristics as close to these criteria as possible.

Before beginning to write, obtain materials from the graduate school that describe format requirements. Obtain recommendations of good dissertations previously approved by members of your committee. Review these theses for ideas on approaches and format. Set a high standard for the work to be written.

Develop a schedule for the dissertation writing and stick to it. Minimize the influences of friends and family during the writing process. This is helped by creating an understanding that the writing time is sacred and necessary for "training" as a scholar. Tricks that help include closing a study door, or having a radio on (if you work well under these conditions), while writing. These actions signal others that you are hard at work.

Deadlines, Typing, and Binding

Graduate schools have several deadlines during the term in which a degree is granted. The thesis abstract has to be in on one date, the first copy of the thesis on another, copyright forms and the final draft of the dissertation on still another date. The worrisome thing about all of these deadlines is that they generally come early in a term. Thus, it is wise to plan a term before the term of graduation to meet the deadlines.

A contract with a typist should be made before the dissertation is begun. Universities employ many secretaries who moonlight. Some graduate student spouses earn supplemental income through dissertation typing. Ask around the department for recommendations. Settle on someone known to be reliable and someone who is emotionally stable.

Expect a bill of several hundred dollars for typing services for a thesis or dissertation. Alternatives include use of a microcomputer with readily available word-processing software. Don't count on the use of a university's central computing facility for word processing. Many institutions have begun to prohibit such usage in lieu of more formidable work. Thus, the microcomputer may be the only option for typing in the near future.

As noted earlier, the abstract is one of the first items that must be deposited with a graduate school. Abstracts of theses and dissertations generally have the following components:

1. Introduction
2. Statement of the problem placed in the context of the discipline
3. Underlying hypotheses
4. Methods used
5. Major findings
6. Short discussion of the novelty and importance of findings, and implications for the field of study

Like the abstract of a research paper, the dissertation abstract can only be written near the end of the dissertation preparation. The dissertation abstract should also be prepared with utmost care because of its impact on committee members and people outside the university after its publication in *Dissertation Abstracts*.

A thesis or dissertation can usually be copyrighted through forms available from the graduate school. This is less important for theses that will be converted into papers for publication in journals than it is for work that may ultimately be published as a book. In the latter case, the copyright gives added protection between the time of acceptance by the graduate school and acceptance by a publisher.

The graduate school is likely to demand at least two bound copies of a thesis or dissertation for deposition in university libraries. Most dissertation committee members do not expect bound copies of theses although it is nice to be able to present one to an advisor.

Oral Examination

In most universities, a committee must approve a thesis or dissertation before it can be accepted by the graduate school. The review process typically involves a one- to three-hour oral exam that requires careful preparation.

The main reason for the oral defense is for the committee to obtain a perspective of the candidate's grasp of the thesis and his or her field of study. This perspective is gained through a range of questions that focus on the contents of the dissertation. The committee may also ask questions in areas of apparent weakness displayed by the candidate during previous research meetings and candidacy exams. Preparation for these questions requires introspection about the candidate's work and her or his academic shortcomings. Physical preparations for the oral include checking the exam room to make sure that audiovisual aids and a blackboard are available.

The oral defense is an open exam. Departmental faculty may be invited by an advisor or department chairman. Candidates may also invite graduate school friends who might welcome a preview of their fate! Seriously, the exam should not be anticipated in foreboding terms. Indeed, consolation should be derived from two thoughts. First, candidates are more knowledgeable than anyone else about their dissertations. Second, while committee members have to satisfy a commitment to scholarship through their questioning, they want to see the candidate succeed. Committee members to varying degrees view a candidate as their student. It is in their interest to see the candidate complete his or her program successfully.

A copy of the thesis or dissertation should be brought to the exam. After greeting the committee members, the chairman will ask the candidate to step outside of the room for a few minutes. During this time, the committee will briefly review the candidate's academic record and agree to rules for the examination. The exam rules will be explained immediately upon the candidate's return. At the start of the exam the chairman may ask the candidate to give a short biographical sketch of herself or himself.

The exam is likely to continue with the candidate being asked to briefly (15 to 20 minutes) review the dissertation. This review should include an honest appraisal of its strengths and weaknesses. Also, the major contributions and implications of the work should be summarized.

Following the review, the chairman will signal the beginning of the questioning. In some cases, the chairman may ask the first question, which can set the tone for the remainder of the exam. However, chairmen of committees I have served on generally relinquish their right of first questioning to prevent allegations of directing the course of an exam. Questions are put forth by each committee member successively. The committee members may refer to specific pages in the candidate's thesis during the questioning. Some questions will be challenging. In fact, I have known chairmen who purposely ask committee members to construct tough questions to assure that the exam ends up as a "memorable experience."

Candidates should not be surprised by questions about their plans for the future and their ideas for publication of the thesis. Committee members may also be interested to learn how the candidate thinks the dissertation contributed to her or his growth as a scholar. Of course, there is often the proverbial question, "If you could remain here a few more years, what problems would you pursue as uncovered by your dissertation?" which is often ironically asked towards the end of the exam when the candidate may be near emotional exhaustion.

After each committee member has had one chance to ask questions, the chairman may call for any further questions at random. When the questioning is completed, the chairman will most likely excuse the candidate but ask him or her to remain nearby. In the candidate's absence, the committee will discuss the exam and the dissertation. A vote will be taken on the outcome. Rules on voting procedures vary among universities, but at minimum, a majority vote will be required for one of the following actions:

1. Unconditional pass with the exception of correction of typographical errors.
2. Conditional pass subject to minor revision.
3. Conditional pass subject to major revision.
4. Failed presentation but passed dissertation.
5. Complete failure.

The third outcome may require additional experiments and writing efforts to satisfy the committee. Outcome four is unusual and easily prevented through the hierarchical system in which a candidate has developed confidence through previous presentations. Outcome five is rare. A complete failure at this stage of a student's career either reflects incompetence on the part of the student *and* advisor, or it is the result of prejudice. In any case, a petitioned review of the student's case would be in order. The decision of a review team as approved by the graduate dean would be final.

In all likelihood, your examination will be successful. The announcement will be received with an extraordinary sense of achievement. Congratulations by each of your committee members will instill a sense of elation as you formally join their ranks and the community of advanced scholars and researchers.

The development of research papers and a dissertation provide opportunities to submit your works to journals or book publishers and to present your research at scientific meetings. These activities are discussed in the next chapter.

Chapter 10

Presentation and Publication of Papers

Nothing clarifies ideas in one's own mind so much as explaining them to other people.
—VERNON BOOTH

The job of the scientist is to discover, confirm, and communicate new knowledge. Writing research papers, as discussed in Chapter 8, is a prerequisite to communication which includes presentations at meetings and publication in journals.

Presentation of Papers at Meetings

Presenting papers at meetings is an important part of the research process. Work is better understood after it has been presented before an audience. Also, the exposure gained through presentation helps researchers meet colleagues who may become important future contacts.

Besides providing contacts, presentations invite criticism. This allows for changes in research directions and new interpretations. Occasionally, compliments will be received. These promote self-confidence and stimulate personal development. Receiving compliments should also prompt one to compliment other deserving scientists. Heightened sensitivity to others' achievements is essential for personal growth and the development of new friendships. Indeed, few things stimulate conversation better than expressed interest in others' work.

Scientific presentations require planning, and they involve the "art of science." It takes imagination and skill to develop good presentations. It also takes the courage of a performer to present one's work before peers. Fortunately, like the work of the artist, the task is eased by practice.

Submission of Abstracts

A paper must first be "accepted" before it can be presented at a sci-

100

entific meeting. This requires the submission of an abstract of the work for review by members of the scientific organization that is sponsoring the meeting. The abstract covers work that is complete but unpublished. The previously discussed guidelines for abstract preparation can be used, but there will be strict length and format requirements. Signatures of sponsors may be required on the abstract form. A second more extensive conference report may have to accompany the abstract. According to Day,[30] the conference report should omit the Introduction, Materials and Methods, Results, and Discussion headings, and be written more like a lengthy abstract. The conference report serves as a truly preliminary report. It can include speculation, alternative theories, and suggestions for future research. The abstract, conference report, and supporting documents may have to be submitted six to nine months before the meeting. Thus, the timely submission of abstracts will take planning and attention to detailed instructions supplied by the sponsoring society or association. An advisor is a good source of guidance on meetings and societies in a discipline.

Types of Presentations

Papers are given at scientific meetings as podium or poster presentations. A podium presentation is typically a 15- to 20-minute oral and visual (i.e., slides) description of work. Poster presentations are visual descriptions of work prepared for poster boards which are displayed for hour-long periods. During the viewing period, the author or authors are available to answer questions or explain the work.

Podium Presentations.   Podium presentations are often frightening to new scientists who fear going blank or erring before an important scientific audience. The chance of this happening, however, can be minimized by planning, hard work, and practice.

Preparation of a good podium presentation starts with a written talk or notes. The written material is prepared from an outline and addresses the following questions:

1. Why was the work done?
2. How was the work done?
3. What was found?
4. What do the results mean?
5. How can the results be summarized, and what do they mean for future experiments?

Answering the first two questions should take about one-third of the presentation. The last two-thirds of the talk should be devoted to the remaining questions, with the bulk of time devoted to questions 3 and 4.

During the write-up, avoid getting bogged down in details. Stick to the salient aspects of the work. Stress those points that will be most important to the audience. Day[30] recommended that an oral presentation be pitched to a more general audience than would read one's publications. Material should be prepared that can comfortably be covered in the time allotted.

Presentations in a foreign language should be prepared for verbatim delivery unless one is fluent in the language. Talks in English should not be read. Alternatively, notes should be prepared on index cards which can be used to guide the presentation. The notes should be typed in large letters. An Orator-Presentor-10 type element available for use with IBM Selectric typewriters is ideal for preparing notes on index cards. The typed cards should be correlated to the slides for the talk—one card per slide.

During the preparation of the presentation outline, ideas will emerge for visual aids. Some of these will include tabular data and figures previously prepared for research reports or papers. As the write-up is revised for the presentation, the functions of visual aids should be considered:

1. *To support the spoken word.* Audience recognition is aided by slides depicting necessary jargon (e.g., geologically important crystals, genera and species of plants and animals, names of diseases).
2. *To amplify the spoken word.* Oral descriptions of periodic, patterned, and cyclical events are supplemented by diagrams. A point may also be emphasized metaphorically by a carefully chosen cartoon.
3. *To replace the spoken word.* Certain conditions or phenomena (e.g., weather patterns, topographical features, trends in data) can be understood only through use of pictures, charts, or graphs.

The visual aids should consist principally of 35 mm or so-called $2''$ $\times$ $2''$ slides. Avoid the old-fashioned $3'' \times 4''$ lantern slides and overhead transparencies. Lantern slide projectors are rarely found at meetings. Overhead projectors are commonly available but may give neither large nor clear enough images for most meeting rooms. Furthermore, most meeting room arrangements do not permit simultaneous use of the podium (where your notes are placed) and the overhead projector, thus making use of the projector awkward. Transparencies may be of limited usefulness off-campus, but they are conveniently used for departmental seminars and research group meetings. Guidelines for use of transparencies and overhead projectors have been developed by Kunka and Kunka.[71]

Veterans of scientific meetings often tell stories of presentations marred by poor slides. Ineffective slides contain one or more of the following faults:

- *Clutter.* Too much is included on the slide. This confuses listeners who may neither decipher nor see material.
- *Poor organization.* Slides are difficult to understand. Too many ideas are presented at once.
- *Poor contrast.* Slides are difficult to read.
- *Distraction.* Slides are prepared with an unusual color or too many colors.

Bauer[7] suggested the KISS method for making slides—"keep it simple stupid!" This brazen charge is meant to emphasize the importance of preparing slides that are the antithesis of those described above. Clutter is prevented by strictly limiting the words on slide plates (sheets containing words, graphs, or other matter to be photographed). This is accomplished by using one of two rectangular templates that can be drawn on a blank sheet of paper. A $9'' \times 6''$ template should be used to prepare slide plates containing a maximum of nine lines centered and spaced $\frac{1}{2}''$ apart. The printing should be no smaller than 18-point and can be prepared with a stencil, press-on letters, or a print-tape machine (Kroy Industries, Stillwater, Minn.). A $4\frac{1}{2}'' \times 3''$ template should be used to prepare slide plates containing a maximum of seven lines centered and spaced $\frac{3}{8}''$ apart. The printing is preferably no smaller than 14-point and can be prepared with the lettering devices noted above. Double-spaced uppercase pica type may also be used with the smaller template, but no more than 45 characters should be typed to the line. Contrast is maximized by typing on high-quality bond paper with a reversed carbon paper and second sheet of paper in that order below the top sheet. The final typed slide plate has typed material on the face and carbon images on the reverse side which improves contrast for photographic processing. Figures and diagrams should be prepared to fit within the $9'' \times 6''$ template. Axes of graphs and other printing should be prepared with 18-point type. All printing and lettering must maximize the black–white contrast of the slide plate. This will prevent poor contrast in the resulting slides.

Figures or diagrams can be outlined with lines and margins drawn in light-blue pencil. The blue lines will not photograph. Graphs from reports or notebooks are copied with tracing paper or traced on typing paper by use of a light box (I²R, Cheltenham, Penn.). Mistakes are corrected with white correction fluid. The final corrected slide plate may appear as a jumble of blue lines and patches of dried correction fluid; however, it should photograph well. This is tested by examination of a photocopy of the plate.

Slide plates should be photographed professionally. This may be done personally with some experience. Techniques for making slides are not difficult to learn (simple instructions have been given by Kemp[69]), but if commercially prepared slides are affordable, time will be saved and a good product will be assured. Furthermore, most university photoservices offer choices of colors and slide mounts. So-called diazo slides provide a white image on a colored background. Blue diazo slides, for example, are commonly used and are easier on an audience's eyes than black-on-white or white-on-black slides. Other diazo colors include brown, green, purple, and red. The latter three may be distracting, depending on their hues.

Slide mounts may be cardboard, plastic, or metal. Sample slides prepared by local photoservice people should be examined. Consider cost and the quality of the mount chosen. Some cardboard and plastic mounts are so flimsy that the film buckles. This can cause annoying unevenness in projected images. The problem is remedied by mounting film between thin glass sheets which are subsequently mounted in plastic or metal.

Prepared slides should be viewed with a projector to determine clarity and projected size. Another simple test is to hold a slide at arm's length before a light source. If the slide is easily read, it is likely to project well before an audience. If not, larger lettering or different contrasting colors may be needed.

Once the notes and slides are complete, practice presentations should be given. Begin by mentally going through the talk several times. Try this during trivial tasks such as bathing, riding public transportation, or waiting for an appointment. When the talk is nearly memorized, ask an advisor and some friends to listen to two or three mock presentations. During the practice presentations try to:

- Speak directly to the listeners and establish eye contact.
- Use notes effectively – do not read from them.
- Vary your tone of voice and watch pronunciation; do not lower your voice at the end of sentences.
- Take time with thought transitions. Try to minimize verbal crutches such as "a" and "you know." A good way to break this habit is to pause and take a breath through your mouth.
- Display some animation with your body and arms, but avoid needless or repetitive gesturing and pacing.
- Show enthusiasm for your work.

After the practice presentations solicit comments and questions. The resulting discussions will help you anticipate inquiries that may arise during the meeting presentation.

The presentation should now be ready to be given at a scientific meeting. On the day of the presentation, arrive early at the meeting room to survey lighting, podium placement, and other arrangements. Make sure that the slides are loaded properly into the projector. This is the speaker's responsibility even if a projectionist is in charge.

There are some aspects of the actual presentation that cannot be anticipated, including the exact composition of the audience and unavoidable nervousness. These factors should not be allowed to defeat you. Avoid telling the audience that you are nervous or that you feel ill-prepared. The listeners came to learn, not to feel sorry for someone. Begin the talk as it was practiced. Try not to fidget or adjust your clothing through the presentation. Three or four steps can be taken on either side of the podium to break tension and refocus your concentration. If you seem to go blank during the presentation, try not to panic. Take a few steps, take a deep breath through your mouth, and direct your eyes away from the audience as you mentally concentrate. Your train of thought should return quickly. Alternatively, you can glance at a copy of your complete paper with key phrases underlined. As a last resort, a sentence or two can be read verbatim from the paper. This is not recommended for routine use, but some people feel less nervous by having their paper nearby. Remember that the audience has no idea what was going to be said. If you stumble slightly or forget a few words, no one is going to punish you. Everyone in the audience was in your shoes at one time, and many will recall that they did a poorer job during their early presentations.

The time should be watched carefully during a presentation. If you forget a wristwatch, watch for clues from the chairman of the session. Rising motions or worried glances are signals that time has expired. Respect timing lights or buzzers that may be used by the meeting organizers.

When the presentation is finished, thank the audience for their attention and indicate a willingness to answer questions. Repeat questions posed by members of the audience; then answer them honestly and succinctly. If you don't know the answer to a question, or a question addresses something that has not been done, answer forthrightly.

Sometimes, listeners become emotional about points raised by talks. Remember that science requires critical appraisal and most researchers can be critical of work without getting personal. Thus, criticism should be taken in the spirit of free inquiry. Occasionally, however, a questioner displays poor manners and may become personally abusive. This is uncalled for and should be addressed properly by the session chairman.

After the question and answer period, thank the audience again and return to your seat. Enjoy the exhilaration of having successfully completed a presentation.

Poster Presentations.   Poster sessions have been used at scientific meetings in the United States since the early 1970s. They were developed as a way of accommodating greater numbers of papers at meetings. A two-hour poster session, for example, can include 25 poster presentations, whereas only six to eight podium presentations would fit into the same time period.

The preparation of posters places special responsibility on the author(s). Posters must stand on their own—a story must be told without explanation. Actually, there is an interesting paradox between the quality of a poster and the inquiries it generates. The informative poster will stimulate questions and discussions. A poster that is poorly organized and technically inferior will repel onlookers.

Plan the posters well. Begin by determining from the meeting organizers the size poster boards that will be available. Typical boards are 4 × 8 feet. The poster should contain:

1. Title, names of authors, and their affiliation—this is placed on a banner that spans the top of the poster
2. Abstract
3. Plates for:
   a. Objectives
   b. Methods
   c. Results
   d. Discussion
   e. Conclusions

The different sections of the poster should be grouped as indicated in Figure 9. Notice that the sections are arranged so that onlookers can quickly grasp an overall impression of the work.

Poster plates are prepared to meet the guidelines discussed under podium presentations. More detail can be added to poster plates, but it is best to keep them as simple as possible. Once the poster plates are made, prepare photographic enlargements measuring about 8 × 10 inches. Lettering should result that is no less than 4 to 5 millimeters in height. Lines for graphs and tables should be no less than 2 millimeters wide. Curves on graphs can be done in different colors by using self-adhesive colored tapes (Chartpak, Leeds, Mass.). The prescribed enlargements should be readable from 8 feet. The title banner can also be made from photographic enlargements, but individual letters should be 3 to 4 inches in height to be readable from 16 feet. Photographic work should be done with high-contrast film. Printing can be on glossy paper, though MacGregor[77] recommended a matte or pearl-surfaced finish to minimize glare. The pearl-surfaced photos are also less prone to curling. Photographs can be mounted on colored construction paper with a non-water-based glue to prevent wrinkling. Glue sticks are conveniently used

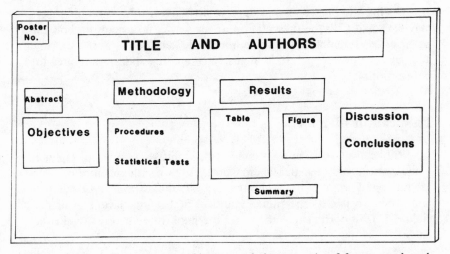

Figure 9   Typical arrangement of banner and plates on a 4 × 8 foot poster board
($^9/_{16}$ inch = 1 foot).

for this purpose. Different-colored backings can be used for each section of the poster. This helps to guide the eyes of onlookers.

After all of the poster materials have been prepared, lay them out on the floor and develop an organized and pleasing arrangement for the plates. Ask an advisor and some friends to view the poster and make comments. After settling on an arrangement, photograph it and use the photograph to duplicate the poster at the meeting. While preparing for the meeting, collect items that will be needed for the poster presentation. These include $^5/_8$-inch steel push pins and a repair kit consisting of an assortment of press-on letters, a single-edged razor blade, extra push pins, a black magic marker, and cellophane tape. Photocopies of an abstract or other relevant materials may be taken to hand out to interested visitors.

On the day of the poster presentation, arrive at least 30 minutes before the scheduled presentation to set up the poster. Be sure to be present at the poster during the appointed times. If there is the option of staying for the entire time the poster is displayed, take it! The more personal contact you have with onlookers the better. Indeed, this is probably one of the greatest advantages of poster presentations over podium presentations.

Encourage questions from serious onlookers by offering to give additional information. Display enthusiasm during discussions of your work with visitors. Don't be afraid to greet and visit with friends who drop by, but try not to monopolize significant blocks of time with chit-chat. Also, try to keep all discussions at a reasonable sound level.

During the poster session observe difficulties that some onlookers may have had with the presentation of the work. Take notes on how the next poster presentation might be improved. Remove the poster on time and save the poster materials for use in preparing slides, or figures for publication.

Publication of Papers

Publication customs vary among disciplines. In some disciplines, graduate students seek publication on their own either before or after graduation. For most fields, however, joint publications with advisors and other workers is the rule. Regardless of the practices in your discipline, it is important to understand the publication process, which includes:

1. Selection of a journal and publisher
2. Preparation of manuscript for publication
3. Submission of manuscript
4. Response to reviews
5. Handling galley and page proofs
6. Ordering reprints and handling page charges
7. Referring to unpublished work
8. Responding to reprint requests

Selecting Journals and Publishers

There are many journals in most fields of science. A survey of *Current Contents* will lead to many titles. The journals found will vary in quality, the most respected generally being those that are published by major societies and associations. Nevertheless, there are some very good journals published by university departments and independent publishers.

Researchers' careers get their greatest boosts from publishing in the best journals. The better journals, however, have rejection rates as high as 90 percent which may cause scientists to shy away from them. This is unfortunate because one or two solid publications in a prestigious journal may be worth as much as five to ten papers in second-rate journals. The lesson for choosing a journal for a manuscript is clear. Select the most prestigious journals, and narrow the choice by considering comparative circulations. Data on circulation are found on the last few pages of the November and December issues of journals, listed in the "Statement of Ownership, Management and Circulation." Another factor to consider is the cost of publication. Some journals charge $50 to $100 a page to publish papers. Also, a processing fee of $25 or more may be assessed when the paper is submitted. Acceptance is not contingent on payment of page charges, but this payment may be expected except under unusual circumstances. Unless an advisor has budgeted for this cost, it is important to consider whether publication in a journal with page charges is worth the cost.

In some fields it is common to publish dissertations as books, but finding a publisher can be difficult. Many commercial publishing firms avoid dissertation manuscripts because their narrow scope can lead to poor sales of resulting books and little profit. For this reason, university presses should be considered. Their purpose is the advancement of knowledge rather than profit, and one is more likely to find publishers of dissertation topics among their ranks. A directory of university presses that indicates preferences for manuscripts in particular fields[1] should be consulted to make a list of possible choices. A priority order can be developed based on the prestige of representative universities.

Preparation of Manuscripts

The purpose, scope, and format of papers for journals are detailed in notices to authors which are published at least once a year. Use guidelines in the notice to authors as well as those in Chapter 8 to prepare the final draft. If a book-length manuscript is planned, obtain the publisher's handbook for authors, which will give details on format. If a paper is being prepared for camera-ready copying, the format guidelines will be extensive and must be reviewed carefully with the secretary typing the paper.

The question of authorship should be discussed before a final draft of a paper is written. In some fields, it is common for graduate students to publish their dissertation research alone. Graduate students in most disciplines, however, publish jointly with their advisor and other faculty or students who are significant contributors to the work. Multiple authorship raises the question of whose name will appear first on the manuscript. This is an important question because modern citation, retrieval, and literature-scanning services can attribute disproportionate credit to the first author. In my research group, first authorship is based on who is credited with the major ideas in the paper and the write-up. Thus, beginning graduate students typically assume a second or third author status. Advanced students often earn first authorship.

Whether the manuscript is book-length or a two-page communication, care should be taken to make sure that it is neat and free from misspellings and typographical errors. This requires careful reading and rereading by all authors. Editors and reviewers are favorably impressed by neatness and correctness. Attention to these details indicates a feeling for aesthetics and an appreciation of good work.

Submitting Manuscripts to Publishers

Prepare a cover letter to accompany the submittal of a manuscript to a publisher. Address the letter to an editor indicated in the notice to authors and include:

1. A statement identifying the contents of the correspondence; e.g., original plus prescribed number of copies of manuscript
2. How the paper should be considered, i.e., as an article, note, or communication
3. A statement indicating that the content of the paper has neither been published nor submitted or accepted for publication by another journal
4. Name and address of recipient of future correspondence if they are different from those of the author of the letter
5. Suggested names (with addresses) of potential reviewers if the paper covers work in a specialized area
6. A simple note of thanks for considering the manuscript

Book-length works should never be sent to publishers without prior approval. If possible, publishers should be visited to discuss projects.

Papers or book-length manuscripts should be bound carefully in manila envelopes and sent by first-class mail to editors. Enclose the prescribed number of copies and include a self-addressed stamped envelope for notice of receipt if this is customary with the publisher. Also include a voucher for payment of review charges if necessary.

Be sure to retain a photocopy of all materials sent to the publisher. For multi-author papers it is proper to supply each author with a copy of the material mailed.

Manuscript Reviews

Word should be obtained that a manuscript has been received and sent out for review by the publisher within two to three weeks of submittal. If no word is received within three weeks, call or write the editorial office to confirm receipt. A report on the review(s) of manuscripts submitted to journals should be received within six to eight weeks. Book-length manuscripts may take four to six months. Few papers are accepted outright, but a paper might be deemed acceptable with minor changes. Alternatively, the reviewer(s) may raise significant questions about the work that will have to be addressed effectively to prompt reevaluation by the editor(s). This may require considerable revision and retyping.

All criticisms of reviewers should be considered seriously and addressed properly during the revision process. The reviews of two or more referees may have notations (e.g., A, B, . . .) that should be referred to in the cover letter. If no notation is given, assign numbers or letters appropriately. Changes should be clearly described in a response by page–paragraph–sentence number citations which are given to help the editor or reviewer locate the revised material. This is effectively done by using different-colored ink to underline new or revised sections of the resubmitted paper. The underlining can be correlated to colors assigned to different reviewers.

Sometimes, footnotes can be used beneficially to respond to reviewer criticism. I have used footnotes such as, "One referee suggested that . . ." to describe a reviewer's concern and to lead into a response.

The revised manuscript and a letter outlining revisions should be returned to the editors. Be sure to include in the letter the manuscript's number as assigned by the editor. If the requests for changes are minor and the objections have been satisfactorily addressed, the editor may exercise her or his prerogative to approve publication. Reviewer requests for major revision, however, may prompt the editor to forward the revised manuscript to the referee(s) for a second review. The reviewer's advice will then be considered by the editor in making a final decision. The time from resubmittal to receipt of word on the manuscript's fate should be within four weeks. Take delight in an acceptance. Alternatively, the manuscript may be rejected at this stage or after the first review.

Editors and publishers are receptive to appeals for reconsideration, but rejection of a revised manuscript is final. A rejection notice received after initial review may contain words of hope such as, "Because the criticisms raised by the reviewer are of a fundamental nature, we regret to inform you that we are unable to accept this paper for publication in the *Journal of Scientific Research*. If it is possible to revise the paper to overcome the reviewer's criticisms, we may reconsider it." Other rejections may offer no hope for reconsideration.

Sometimes, rejections are based on factors other than scientific soundness. Consider this one: "Your paper which you kindly submitted for publication has been reviewed by an outside referee and a member of our Editorial Board. They believe that it is likely to be of interest primarily to a narrow range of specialists and it is therefore unsuitable for publication in the *Journal*. I regret that we cannot accept it."

Rejection letters are received by the best of scientists. Appropriate responses to rejection notices are to evaluate the scientific basis for criticisms, revise the work accordingly, and seek another journal or publisher. Veteran writers will confess to receiving numerous rejection notices, but

© 1981 United Feature Syndicate, Inc.

for many of the manuscripts that were initially reviewed unfavorably, ultimate publication resulted in rave reviews or scores of reprint requests. Occasionally, reviews reveal fatal flaws in work that make it unsuitable for publication. The above situations characterize the publishing world, and it is important for researchers to develop the sense of tenacity that is necessary to survive in it.

Handling Proofs

Manuscripts that are typeset go through a proofing stage. The process involves review and revision of typeset material on legal-sized sheets known as galley proofs. It is the author's responsibility to peruse galley proofs for errors introduced during typesetting and to make changes using proofreaders' marks (Table 11), the uses of which are exemplified in Figure 10. Galley proofs may also contain questions from

Table 11 Proofreaders' marks and margin instructions for printers[a]

Instruction	Mark in text	Mark in margin
Capitalize	Hela cells	*cap*
Make lower case	the Penicillin reaction	*l.c.*
Delete	a ~~very~~ good reaction	
Close up	Mac Donald reaction	
Insert space	lymph node cells	#
Start new paragraph	in the cells. The next	
Insert comma	in the cells after which	
Insert semicolon	in the cells however	
Insert hyphen	well known event	=
Insert period	in the cells Then	⊙
Insert word	in cells	# *the* #
Transpose	proofreader	*tr*
Subscript	CO2	
Superscript	32P	
Set in roman type	The *bacterium* was	*rom*
Set in italic type	P. aeruginosa cells	*ital*
Set in boldface type	Results	*b.f.*
Let it stand	a ~~very~~ good reaction	*stet*

[a] From R. A. Day, How to write and publish a scientific paper, 2nd ed., p. 98, ISI Press, Philadelphia, 1983. Reprinted by permission of the publisher.

editors. These author queries should be answered succinctly in the margins.

The production of proofs of papers may be close to the time for printing; thus, proofreading should be completed within 48 hours. Avoid making revisions in the copy unless they are absolutely necessary. Author-initiated changes at the galley proof stage can delay publication and may result in a charge for services.

I have composed this paragraph to show you how proofreaders' marks are used on galley or page proofs. You should note special instructions that may be given by the publisher on the use of english, technical expressions, etc. Also, the proofs may contain questions that should be answered succinctly in ~~the~~ margins. Try to return the corrected proofs within 48 hours to the *printer*. Be sure to note the correct address of the printer however, it may be the same as that of the publisher.

Figure 10 Examples of the use of proofreaders' marks and margin instructions.

The corrected proofs should be returned by first-class mail to the printer. Be careful to note the printer's address. It is frequently different from that of the editor or publisher.

The proofing of book-length manuscripts cannot be completed in 48 hours. The printer, however, is likely to have a deadline and may ask that you expedite the proofing step. One or two weeks is a typical allotment for this task.

Requests for purchase orders for reprints and page charges will often accompany galley proofs. An advisor will have to approve these purchases from a university account, and it will take some prognosticating to anticipate reprint needs. Until publication, an accepted paper may be referred to as *in press* or *accepted for publication* in interim papers or reports. Before acceptance, papers are referred to as *unpublished results* (in footnotes or parentheses) and are usually excluded from bibliographies.

Acceptance and publication of the first paper are important milestones in the career of a scientist. Seeing one's name in print provides the thrill experienced by performers who see their "name in lights." The experience with reprints of a researcher's first paper has been aptly described by Slobodkin[116]: "Reprints of his first published paper are sent to parents and grandparents; and the first reprint requests from strangers in Iowa or, better still, from agricultural stations in India or Brazil produce a tremendous elation."

Presentation and publication are terminating points in research projects. Many of these projects, however, require earlier attention to special populations (e.g., animals, human subjects) or unusual handling procedures (e.g., biohazards). These topics are covered in the next chapter.

Chapter 11

Research with Human Subjects, Animals, and Biohazards

Many of the problems facing us may be soluble,
but only if we are willing to embrace brilliant,
daring and complex solutions. Such solutions
require brilliant, daring and complex people.
— CARL SAGAN

Scientists and researchers operate under three suppositions: (1) research is beneficial to society; (2) researchers are benevolent and trustworthy; (3) scientific research is non-political. The ethical correlates to these tenets are: (1) research is justified by its benefits; (2) researchers should be principally responsible for the conduct of research; (3) researchers should be self-governing and self-regulating. Unfortunately, history attests to exceptions to these ideals that have led to regulations. These are promulgated by government bodies, and the regulations are generally as interesting to read as telephone directories. Historical perspectives and interpretive reviews are needed to help investigators comply with federal regulations on research with human subjects, animals, and biohazards (i.e., radioactive materials, toxic chemicals, and dangerous drugs).

Human Subjects Research

Research with human subjects plays an indispensable role in the biomedical and social–behavioral sciences. In human subjects research, however, there is a counterplay between benefits derived and the risks to subjects.

115

Historical Background

As noted by Brady and Jonsen,[18] human experimentation predates the first century A.D. when Egyptian physicians were known to "engage" convicted criminals in vivisection experiments. Many centuries passed before English and German literary movements in the late eighteenth and early nineteenth centuries produced works that served as a portent of concern for human subjects in research. Mary Shelley's *Frankenstein*, for example, warns scientists about placing research goals above human feeling.

The second half of the nineteenth century witnessed the development of scientific rationalism and the industrial revolution. This was accompanied by a rise in Western Individualism that has been characterized by Joseph Brady[17] as an ". . . autonomous challenge to paternalistic practices which were previously assumed to be beneficial to the individual." Simultaneously, there was a shift away from the concept of the physician as strictly a provider of primary care. A sense emerged that the physician had the responsibility to develop knowledge for the benefit of others.

The three research suppositions noted earlier seemed to function for human subjects research through the 1940s. After World War II, however, descriptions of Nazi experiments with human beings shocked and horrified humanity. The world could no longer rely on the a priori benevolence of researchers.

To provide a basis for conviction of the Nazi criminals during the Nuremberg Trials, the United States Military Tribunal developed a set of guidelines for conducting human experimentation. Briefly, these rules stated that: (1) voluntary consent by subjects is essential; (2) subjects cannot be used except when research results can be obtained in no other way and when prior animal studies indicate that disability or death will not occur; (3) the expected benefits must outweigh the risks; (4) only qualified investigators will conduct research; (5) subjects can withdraw at will; (6) research is terminated if risks increase during experimentation.

After the Nuremburg Trials, the World Medical Association and medical societies in the United States and the United Kingdom adopted ethical codes worded similarly to the above recommendations. Despite these commitments and the requirement of consent forms mandated by the 1962 amendments to the 1938 Food, Drug and Cosmetic Act, serious violations of human rights continued in biomedical experimentation through the early 1960s.

In 1966, Beecher[8] documented 22 examples of studies published in reputable medical journals that revealed serious breaches in ethics. Included in the Beecher article were the infamous Willowbrook Study and what became known as the (New York) Jewish Chronic Disease Hospital Case. In the Willowbrook study, infectious hepatitis was induced in mentally defective children. While the parents gave consent to injection or oral administration of the virus, they were not informed of the hazards involved. In the Jewish Chronic Disease Hospital case, live cancer cells were injected into 22 human subjects as part of a study of immunity to the disease. The subjects were just told that they ". . . would be receiving some cells. . . ."; the word "cancer" was not used.

In the 1960s, experiments in social psychology involving deceit came under attack by social–behavioral scientists, ethicists, and governmental administrators. As noted by Hunt,[61] the indignation was principally against work published by Stanley Milgram at Yale in 1963. Milgram instructed naive subjects to administer progressively more powerful electric shocks to an unseen confederate linked to the subject by intercom. The subjects were directed to continue the administration of "shocks" even after mock grunts, cries, and screams were heard. Milgram reported that a number of operatives "were observed to sweat, tremble, stutter, bite their lips, groan, and dig their fingernails into their flesh"; yet, most of them obeyed Milgram's orders. Milgram justified his work on the basis of developing an understanding of normal human behavior. Ironically, this type of behavior contributed to excesses in Nazi Germany during the 1930s and 1940s.

Milgram's experiments, the Beecher article, and finally, revelations in the early 1970s of the Tuskegee study, all influenced subsequent federal legislative action.

The Tuskegee case originated in the 1930s when the U.S. Public Health Service began studying the long-term effects of syphilis in men. Two groups of black men were chosen for the investigation which was conducted at a penal institution in Tuskegee, Alabama. One group had syphilis; the second was disease free. Through the next 30 years, the men were given normal health care but no treatment for syphilis. Thus, the study extended well into the time when antibiotics were available for effective treatment of syphilis.

Americans were shocked by the Tuskegee study. Congress reacted by passage of the National Research Act (Public Act 93-348) which was signed into law on July 12, 1974. This act provided for interim regulations for the conduct of biomedical and social–behavioral research. Simultaneously, the National Commission for the Protection of Human Subjects of Biomedical and Behavioral Research was established. The Commission's 1979 report, popularly referred to as the Belmont Report[9] (after an intensive series of discussions held in the Smithsonian Institution's Belmont Conference Center) was well received and became the basis for amended regulations[24] that are now in force.

Current Regulations

The Federal Regulations for human subjects research[24] are applicable only to federally sponsored research. Under the "principle of preemption," states, municipalities, and other bodies may not pass laws that lessen the impact of federal statutes. Lower legislative bodies and universities through institutional policy may, however, augment federal laws with their own rules and regulations. Thus, researchers must find out all the regulations for human subjects research that apply at their institutions. Fortunately, the composite rules are contained in a university's Institutional General Assurance (IGA). IGAs are approved by the Department of Health and Human Services (DHHS) [National Institutes of Health, Office for Protection from Research Risks (OPRR), Westwood Building, Room 3A-18, Bethesda, MD 20205, (301) 496-7004] as a basis for regulating human subjects research at institutions that accept federal funds. This includes practically all institutions of higher learning in the United States.

It is important to obtain a copy of a university's IGA (or its equivalent) through the university's sponsored-research office. After the IGA has been read, questions can be directed to staff of the sponsored-research office or to the chairman of a university's Institutional Review Board (IRB) (see below).

The IGA commits an institution to policy and procedures that assure that subjects do not engage in research without being properly informed. Informed consent involves the following characteristics:

1. *Information.* Subjects are given information on procedures, possible benefits, risks, and investigators as necessary to make judgments about participation.
2. *Understanding.* Investigators take measures to assure that subjects understand the consequences of participation in the research.
3. *Voluntariness.* Subjects are given opportunities to contemplate their decision to participate, and they give consent without coercion and with the understanding that they may withdraw at any time.

The informed consent procedure must be carefully designed and administered. Its completion is documented by a consent form. The consent form, therefore, is principally a legal instrument designed to protect the investigator and the institution. Guidelines for the preparation of consent forms are given in Appendix 3.

Some social science researchers employ deception. That is, if valid experiments are to be conducted, the subject cannot be informed of all elements of the research. Investigators argue that without this deception they cannot accurately assess human behavior since subjects might modify their actions according to what they think is expected. An extreme example of deception is Milgram's "shock" experiments described earlier. While experiments like this are unlikely to be approved under current regulations, research involving deception is approvable under the following conditions:

1. Deception is necessary and alternative procedures are not available.
2. The deceptive procedure will not place subjects at significant physical, psychological, social, or financial risk.
3. The experiments are followed by careful debriefing sessions where the subjects are fully informed.

Certain types of research are considered innocuous enough to be exempted from IRB review.[24] These categories of research include:

1. Research conducted in established or commonly accepted educational settings and research that involves normal educational practices.
2. Research involving the use of educational tests (cognitive, diagnostic, aptitude, achievement) if information taken from these sources is recorded so that subjects cannot be identified.
3. Research involving survey or interview procedures, except where all of the following conditions exist:
   a. responses are recorded so that human subjects can be identified, directly or through identifiers linked to the subjects;
   b. the subject's responses, if they become known outside the research, could place the subject at risk of criminal or civil liability or be damaging to the subject's financial standing;
   c. the research deals with sensitive aspects of the subject's own behavior.
4. Research involving the observation (including observation by participants) of public behavior, except where all of the following conditions exist;
   a. observations are recorded so that the human subjects can be identified;
   b. the observations recorded about the individual, if they became known outside the research, could place the subject at risk;
   c. the research deals with sensitive aspects of the subject's own behavior.
5. Research involving the collection or study of existing data, documents, records, pathological specimens, or diagnostic specimens, if these sources are publicly available or if the information is recorded so that subjects cannot be identified.

The "principle of preemption" applies to the exemptions, and it should be determined whether a university's IGA prescribes stricter rules.

Whether exempted or IRB-reviewed (see below) research is conducted, it is wise and ethically appropriate to make sure that subjects are as informed as possible.

Institutional Review Boards

Society recognizes the importance of human subjects research. It also strives to protect the powerless. Subjects enlisted in studies are generally naive about the research process. Their participation may be the first activity of its type in their lives. These individuals deserve the protection of informed consent and peer review. The peer review process is accomplished through an IRB.

An IRB is a committee appointed by a university administrator responsible for research (e.g., vice president for research or equivalent). The IRB has the following makeup[24]:

- At least five members of varying background and expertise
- Neither all men nor all women, or members entirely from one profession
- At least one member from a non-scientific area (e.g., law, ethics or theology)
- At least one member who is not affiliated with the institution or is not a member of a family of an employee of the institution

The IRB's chief responsibility is to decide whether research projects place subjects at risk, and if so, will:

- the risks be outweighed by the benefits to the subject and the knowledge to be gained from the study?
- the rights and welfare of subjects be adequately protected?
- ethically appropriate and legally effective informed consent be secured from subjects?

Considerations of research purpose and design are not directly at issue in these judgments. If a proposal is scientifically flawed so that no valid conclusions can be reached, however, then it behooves the IRB to reject the proposal based on a poor risk/benefit ratio. The IRB also has the authority to institute monitoring systems to ensure the rights and welfare of subjects.

IRBs meet according to guidelines set forth in IGAs. Generally, meetings are held once or twice a month. Prior to their meeting, the IRB members should receive copies of the proposals they are to consider from investigators. Sponsored projects office staff know when the IRB meets and what type of documentation is necessary for the review process. Usu-

"There are no great men, my boy—only great committees."

Cartoon by Chas. Addams © 1975, The New Yorker Magazine, Inc.

ally, a proposal synopsis will have to be prepared by the investigator. The synopsis accompanies the protocol and contains information such as:

1. Requirements for the subject population and, if applicable, the rationale for using special groups such as prisoners, children, the mentally infirm, or groups whose ability to give voluntary consent may be impaired.
2. Potential risks—physical, psychological, social, or legal, their seriousness, and the likelihood of their occurrence. If there are potential risks, other methods should be described that were considered and indications given why these methods will not be used.
3. The consent procedures to be followed, including how and when informed consent will be obtained, and an explanation if consent will not be obtained.

4. Procedures, including confidentiality safeguards, for protecting against and minimizing risks, and a description of their likely effectiveness.
5. The potential benefits to be gained by subjects, and benefits that may accrue to society as a result of the planned investigation.
6. The risk/benefit ratio and an explanation of how it was computed.

Note that the proposal synopsis contains many of the concerns considered under the former discussions on informed consent and the preparation of a consent form. Thus, the preparation of all three items should be done at the same time.

Often a proposal can be submitted to a funding agency before it is reviewed by the IRB. This assumes, of course, that the review will occur prior to a decision on funding. For example, the National Institutes of Health (NIH) permits submittal of non-reviewed proposals. The IRB, however, must approve or reconcile any points of contention between the investigator and the committee within 60 days of submittal. If irreconcilable differences exist or the proposal is disapproved, it must be withdrawn from the NIH. Some universities require that the review process be completed before a proposal leaves campus. It is important to find out the procedure used at an institution. If this is not done, time may be wasted by an inability to meet a submittal deadline.

Some universities have a two-tiered review system. Proposals must be reviewed at the departmental level before being considered by the IRB. Alternatively, certain types of proposals may only require review at the departmental level. The IGA or the chairmen of the departmental committee and of the IRB are good sources of information on procedures and regulations.

A typical procedure for preparing human subject research protocols might be as follows:

1. Develop the research hypothesis.
2. Design the study and prepare the proposal, taking into consideration:
   a. the procedures for informed consent
   b. the consent form
   c. the synopsis of the proposal.
3. Obtain counsel through the departmental review committee or its equivalent (e.g., departmental research committee).
4. Submit the proposal to IRB for review.

If an IRB or departmental review committee requests changes in the human subject protection aspects of a proposal, requests should be clarified before proceeding. Also, the action necessary to document the changes should be determined. Researchers should not be afraid to seek information and advice from committee chairmen or members. In the process, determine whether it is customary for investigators to attend department or IRB meetings convened to review a protocol. A visit with an IRB is also helpful when communications between an investigator and the committee have been difficult. IRB members are researchers, and they understand the struggles necessary to comply with regulations. Good investigators empathize with their subjects and appreciate the need for regulations. This is best understood by being a subject yourself in research — a role that should be played by all human subjects researchers at some time.

A sense of satisfaction is felt once a researcher has had a protocol approved by an IRB. Once that happens, however, the major accountability for the rights and welfare of subjects falls on the researcher's shoulders. Researchers must see that protocols are followed properly. If problems arise, it is the researcher's responsibility to inform the IRB promptly. Few research activities involve greater responsibilities and professional acumen than those involving human subjects.

Use of Animals in Research

The importance of animals in research can be traced to the late eighteenth century when scientists began to use animals for models to study human illnesses. Edward Jenner in 1798, for example, used a cowpox preparation to inoculate humans against smallpox after discovering a low incidence of smallpox in milkmaids. Robert Koch and Louis Pasteur used animals during the latter part of the 1800s to elucidate the correlation between "germ" exposure and diseases. The famous canine experiments of Banting and Best in the 1920s helped to determine a cause for diabetes mellitis in mammals. The latter work was a portent of the extensive use of animal experimentation in biomedical research during the following 60 years.

The use of animals in behavioral research began in the early part of the twentieth century when investigators at Clark University in Worcester, Massachusetts, studied the behavior of white rats placed in mazes, in problem boxes, and on revolving drums. In 1915 animal behavioral psychology received its first serious recognition as a subdiscipline. In that year, John B. Watson was elected president of the American Psychological Association. Watson's influential book, *Behavior: An Introduction to Comparative Psychology*, [131] was published a year earlier and served as a basis for the extensive animal-based psychological and ethological research that would follow.

Humane Treatment of Animals

Human interest in animals dates back to ancient times. Fondness for animals led to domestication, which first occurred over 3,000 years ago. Humans also seem to have a propensity for cruelty towards animals. This probably has its roots in the various teachings about the dominion of humans over the earth. Frucht[52] noted that early anthropocentric Christian theology, supported by Roman Law, led to the attitude that humans had neither moral nor legal obligations to animals because they lack immortal souls. With the Renaissance, social activists, particularly in England, began to speak out against cruelty to animals. The early nineteenth-century British artist and social critic William Hogarth castigated society for animal cruelty and suggested that it tore at the fabric of humanity.

Goodrich[57] and French[51] noted that antivivisectionist movements in nineteenth-century England captured the sympathy of Queen Victoria, who formed a Royal Commission and charged it with the study of animal cruelty during experimentation. The recommendations of the Commission led to the Cruelty to Animals Act of 1876 which is essentially in force today. This legislation, however, did not satisfy more radical antivivisectionist elements that became influential in both England and the United States through the turn of the century.

The intent of most antivivisectionist groups throughout the twen-

© Sidney Harris

tieth century has been the ban of all animal experimentation. Unfortunately, some biomedical researchers have reacted defensively. In recent years, however, noted scientists from various fields have sought a position between the antivivisectionists and researchers who display inadequate concern for animal sensitivities. Sagan[113] and Pratt[103] have warned about human chauvinism and have called for a greater awareness of animal rights. Collectively, these individuals recognize a behavioral corollary to Darwinian evolution—a spectrum of emotional awareness and intelligence among different animal species. As noted elegantly in a position paper of the Federation of American Scientists:

> The vested psychic unwillingness of man to admit his resemblance to lower animals must eventually fall before the onslaught both of scientific advance and of rising social conscience. In the light of this new consciousness, all of the many ways, justified and unjustified, in which man exploits his fellow animals will be reexamined. As this time approaches, scientists ought not be aligned solely on behalf of justified exploitation. And where exploitation is required, as in justified experimentation, we ought to be able to show that a defense of these practices can coexist with the ongoing application of live compassion.[46]

Animal Welfare Legislation

After World War II, biomedical research increased markedly in the United States. Antivivisectionist activities and a heightened awareness of animal rights elicited responses from the federal government. A series of surveys of animal research performed by the NIH in the 1960s led to the passage of the Animal Welfare Act of 1967 (and amendments in 1970 and 1976) and publication of a guide for laboratory care that was most recently updated in 1978.[59] The guide contains minimum requirements for handling, maintaining, and transporting live vertebrate animals. Institutions receiving NIH funds for research with animals must submit an assurance document to the OPRR (i.e., the same agency that regulates human subjects research) committing themselves to principles in the guide. All researchers who use animals in research should have a copy of this guide, which is available at nominal cost.

A university's Institutional Assurance requires establishment of an Animal Research Committee (ARC) to oversee animal research activities on campus. The ARC has at least five members whose experience and background qualify them for the oversight function. At least one member must be a veterinarian who is also likely to be administratively responsible for animal welfare at the institution (e.g., Director of Animal Resources Center). Like human subjects research regulations, animal research guidelines can be strengthened by state or local statutes and by university policy. The chairman of the ARC can supply a copy of an institution's guidelines.

The guiding principles of animal research are as follows:

Personnel
1. Experiments with live, vertebrate animals and tissues from living animals must be conducted under the supervision of qualified biological, behavioral, or medical scientists.
2. Housing, care, and feeding of experimental animals must be supervised by a qualified veterinarian.

Research
1. Research must be designed to yield results for the good of society. Experiments must not be random or unnecessary.
2. Experiments should be based on knowledge of diseases or problems under study with anticipated results that justify their performance.
3. Mathematical models and *in vitro* biological systems should be used when possible to reduce numbers of animals needed.
4. All unnecessary suffering and injury to animals must be avoided during experimentation.
5. Investigators must terminate experiments when it is believed that continuation may result in unnecessary suffering or injury to animals.
6. If experiments are likely to cause greater discomfort than that attending anesthetization, animals must be treated appropriately with analgesics. The only exception to this is cases where drug treatment defeats the purpose of the experiment and data cannot be obtained by any other humane procedure. Such experiments must be scrupulously supervised by qualified senior scientists.
7. Post-experimental care of animals must minimize discomfort and consequences of any disability resulting from the experiment, in accordance with acceptable veterinary practice.
8. Euthanasia must be accomplished in a humane manner using acceptable practices and insuring immediate death.[107] No animal should be disposed of until death is ascertained.

Facilities and Transportation
1. Standards for construction and use of housing, service, and surgical facilities should meet those described in the guide.
2. Transportation of animals must meet standards and regulations intended to reduce discomfort, stress, and spread of disease.[23] All animals received for experimental purposes must be promptly uncrated and placed in permanent facilities.

Animal Models

If the antivivisectionists prevailed, all animal research would have to be abandoned. We should recognize the importance of finding alternatives (e.g., *in vitro* microbiological or mammalian cell culture procedures, mathematical models) to the use of animals in research. Indeed, federal legislation that authorizes funds for this type of research and private efforts may ultimately yield useful methods. Our current knowledge, however, makes animal research irreplaceable in the advancement of knowledge and the prevention of suffering in humans through advances in biomedical research. Thus, scientists should unequivocally support animal research, but they should also be sensitive to the need for humane treatment of fellow creatures in the animal world.

Veterinary Care and Assistance

Laboratory animal medicine (LAM) has emerged as a specialty of veterinary medicine during the past 30 years. LAM professionals are typically graduate veterinarians who have advanced research degrees or postdoctoral training. The guide[59] and attendant legislation of the Animal Welfare Act require that universities receiving NIH support provide "adequate veterinary care" for animals used in research. This care is generally supplied by a LAM specialist who may also head a centralized animal research facility. Researchers should know the LAM specialist on their campus if they are going to do animal experiments.

The stages of animal research where the LAM specialist contributes are:

1. Procurement of animals
2. Receipt, quarantine, evaluation, and release of animals for experimentation
3. Consultation and collaboration during research

Many universities have central procurement procedures for animals. Paperwork which may have to be prepared by researchers includes information on species, strain, and number of animals needed, as well as descriptions of their proposed use in research. Special instructions for handling and contraindicated procedures may also be requested. The LAM specialist can advise researchers on the proper selection of species or strains, the statistical validity of the numbers of animals proposed for study, and cost factors.

Once animals are received, they are quarantined. The quarantine period permits adjustment to a new environment and recovery from shipping stress. LAM professionals also observe the animals during the quarantine period and perform diagnostic tests. Necessary treatment or vaccinations can be given to prevent introduction of diseases into established colonies. Lang[73] indicated that quarantine periods vary with species but are as follows for common laboratory animals: mouse and rat, 5 days; guinea pig and hamster, 7 days; cat, dog, and rabbit, 14 days; nonhuman primates, 30 days. The lengths of quarantine periods should be considered when estimating elapsed time needed from day of ordering to day of experimentation. Also, an advisor's approval will be necessary before ordering animals. Besides procurement charges, most universities assess a per diem charge for animals to cover feeding, watering, and cage-cleaning costs.

The LAM specialist should be consulted on health and general welfare concerns that arise during experimentation. If animals die unexpectedly during an experiment, it is important that the veterinarian determine whether the cause of death is related to the experimental treatment and take measures to prevent the spreading of infectious diseases when necessary. The LAM specialist can also be considered as a possible collaborator in research projects. The expertise of a veterinary scientist can add considerable strength in many areas of research. This is particularly true in projects requiring surgery, histopathology, chronic treatments, and animal modeling. LAM specialists can also make unique contributions during service on dissertation committees.

Biohazards

Potential or real biohazards include recombinant DNA molecules, etiologic agents (e.g., bacteria, fungi, parasitic agents), oncogenic viruses, and chemicals that are radioactive, or potentially toxic to animals and humans. A variety of federal guidelines or standards exist for the handling and disposal of these agents.

Recombinant DNA Molecules

The first significant research efforts with recombinant DNA material occurred in the early 1970s. As noted by Fredrickson,[50] the short history of recombinant DNA research is marked by controversy. The potential hazards of inserting foreign genetic material in common gut bacteria such as *Escherichia coli* were either overstated or misunderstood. Cautious progress in this field of research has given scientists and federal officials more realistic perspectives that have been used to prepare recently adopted guidelines.[45] These guidelines have less force of law than the regulations governing human and animal research; however, researchers will find that most universities have adopted them.

The guidelines recommend the formation of an Institutional Biosafety Committee (IBC) which oversees the construction and handling of recombinant DNA molecules, and organisms and viruses containing recombinant DNA molecules. In the context of the guidelines, recombinant DNA molecules are (1) molecules constructed outside living cells by joining natural or synthetic DNA segments to DNA molecules which are subsequently replicated in a living cell or (2) DNA molecules replicated as a result of the steps in 1. If a synthetic DNA segment is not expressed *in vivo* yielding a biologically active polynucleotide or polypeptide, then it is exempt from the guidelines.

The IBC consists of no fewer than five members who collectively have expertise in recombinant DNA technology. They must also be capable of assessing the safety of proposed recombinant DNA research and the risks to public health and environment. At least two members of the IBC must not be affiliated with the university and should represent public health and environmental interests of the surrounding community. The IBC on many campuses will be responsible for all biohazards (see below), not just those associated with recombinant DNA molecules.

The IBC's responsibility in recombinant DNA research is to evaluate proposals for potential hazards and to ensure that suitable precautions are adopted. Investigations are divided into four categories:

1. Experiments requiring review and approval by the DHHS Recombinant DNA Advisory Committee (RAC), the NIH, and the IBC
2. Experiments needing IBC review and approval only
3. Experiments that require only notification of the IBC before implementation
4. Experiments exempt from IBC review

Increasingly sophisticated physical containment systems are required for the more potentially dangerous experiments. The physical facilities are categorized as P1, P2, P3, and P4, with P4 involving the most stringent containment. The federal guidelines and university policy statements should be consulted for more extensive descriptions of containment conditions and review procedures, respectively. The IBC chairman is a good source of information and advice. He or she may also provide an institutional policy statement that should be consulted if work is planned with any biohazardous materials.

Microbiological Hazards

Etiologic agents and oncogenic viruses are two other biohazards that require special handling. Federal regulations have not been promulgated in these areas though standards have been published by the Center for Disease Control[22] and the National Cancer Institute[34,92] that merit review if a researcher's work involves these agents.

Radiation Hazards, Toxic Chemicals, and Dangerous Drugs

The use of devices emitting ionizing radiation or radioactive materials, toxic chemicals, and dangerous drugs in research requires unique rules and regulations. Universities often employ safety officers who have oversight responsibilities. It is important to locate these individuals for relevant documents on university rules and policies.

The radiation safety officer may serve under the auspices of a radiation safety committee (RSC) which will be appointed through a central administrative office (e.g., president). The radiation safety program devised by the RSC and maintained on a day-to-day basis by the radiation safety officer will likely involve the following functions:

1. Terminate activities causing radiation hazards.
2. Inspect areas where sources of radiation are stored or used in research.
3. Enforce a program of procurement and record keeping required of all authorized users of radioactive sources or materials.
4. Maintain systems for proper disposal of radioactive wastes.
5. Manage ongoing educational programs on safety precautions and procedures. Assure that new radiation sources are kept in compliance with federal and state regulations.
6. Serve as liaison between university officials and federal and state officials to assure fulfillment of radiation safety and licensure requirements.

To use radiation sources or materials, researchers will have to obtain approval through the radiation safety officer. Usually an advisor will be the authorized user who will be given authority to delegate activities to students. This compounds the students' responsibilities and requires that they become well informed. A radiation safety course(s) can be taken through the radiation safety office. A copy of the university's radiation safety manual can also be obtained. Even if one's background is in physics or chemistry, the practical insights gained through a radiation safety course will be valuable.

The university's safety office will also be responsible for the pick-up and disposal of toxic chemicals. It is important to find out what waste containers are to be used for temporary containment. The proper routine for requesting permanent disposal should also be determined. Researchers should assiduously avoid disposal of chemicals in sinks or common sewer drains.

Researchers should know about the biological effects of toxic and carcinogenic chemicals. Standard reference works give useful toxicity data.[32,40,121] Specific guidelines for laboratory use of chemical carcinogens have been issued based on standards promulgated by the Occupational Safety and Health Administration (OSHA) of the Department of Labor.[94] Recommendations for containment and minimization of contact should be in force in relevant laboratories. Briefly, inhalation of toxic chemicals should be minimized through use of fume hoods, and skin and eye contact should be prevented by appropriate coverings.[121] Safety office personnel are usually able to check the efficiency of fume hoods.

Various potent drugs are useful tools in biological research. When the required drugs have a high abuse potential, they may be categorized as Scheduled Drugs by the Drug Enforcement Administration (DEA) of the Department of Justice under the Controlled Substances Act of 1970. Following are examples of drugs or drug-containing dosage forms listed under Schedules I through V, with drugs of greatest abuse potential listed in Schedule I.

Schedule I
    Strongly Addicting Opiate-Type Drugs
        e.g., acetylmethadol, heroin
    Hallucinogenic Drugs
        e.g., lysergic acid diethylamide (LSD), marijuana, mescaline

Schedule II
    Moderately Addicting Opiate-Type Drugs
        e.g., codeine, morphine
    Strongly Stimulant Drugs
        e.g., amphetamine, methylphenidate
    Strongly Depressant Drugs
        e.g., methaqualone, pentobarbital

Schedule III
    Stimulant Drugs
        e.g., chlorphentermine, phendimetrazine
    Depressant Drugs
        e.g., methylprylon, glutethimide

Schedule IV
  Weakly Depressant Drugs
    e.g., chloral hydrate, meprobamate

Schedule V
  Miscellaneous Drugs of Abuse
    e.g., mixtures or pharmaceutical preparations containing not
    more than 200 milligrams of codeine per 100 milliliters

A more complete listing of scheduled drugs is available through the DEA.[31] The use of scheduled substances in laboratory research, excluding humans, requires permission of an authorized user such as an advisor who may be registered by the DEA. Alternatively, internal authorization procedures through the university's safety office may be possible. Regardless of the authorization procedure, scheduled drug use requires strict accounting procedures and security measures. Researchers should make sure they understand all these procedures before taking on responsibilities.

The conduct of special types of research is aided by guidelines in this chapter. These guidelines will also help during the preparation of grant proposals, which is covered in the next chapter.

Chapter **12**

Getting Grant Support

*Grant funds in both the public and private sector are
decreasing and the number of scholars and researchers
applying for them has grown. Grant seekers today must
be prepared to meet powerful competition.*
                                                    —VIRGINIA P. WHITE

Grants provide support for research and scholarly activities. They are
vital to academic life. Graduate students may apply for a grant or work
on one with an advisor; therefore, it is important to know about different
grants and granting agencies.

Historical Background

The word "grant" means a gift such as money, land, or other type
of support. Grants are at least as old as recorded human history.
White[137] notes that an entry in the *Egyptian Book of the Dead* refers
to a good man who gave a boat to one who had none. The gift served
a useful purpose. This is characteristic of grants. Moreover, the ancient
grantor may have benefited occasionally from gifts of fresh fish from the
grantee. Consequently, the grantor could have served self-interest through
the award. This is also characteristic of grants.

Grants may be used to set up endowments for perpetual support of
activities. Plato's Academy was maintained for hundreds of years by his
endowment. The early church used endowments to support schools,
almshouses, orphanages, monasteries, and hospitals. British royalty endowed charter companies such as the East India and Hudson Bay Companies that helped commercial development in colonial America.

The Smithsonian Institution in Washington, D.C., was started
through a grant in 1835 from James B. Smithson, an amateur natural
historian of English birth. The first recorded congressional grant-making

133

act resulted in a $30,000 award to Samuel F. B. Morse in 1842 for testing the feasibility for public use of the electromagnetic telegraph system.[137] Morse worked earlier on the basis for the telegraph, and his investigations serve as precedent for pilot studies that continue to be necessary for effective grantsmanship.

The success of the industrial revolution in the United States during the late 1800s helped develop industrial magnates such as Andrew Carnegie, Henry Ford, and John D. Rockefeller. Their extraordinary accumulations of wealth permitted the establishment of foundations that continue to support research and scholarship in the United States. The total support from foundations, however, is a small part of the total research and development budget of American universities.

The federal government was a poor supporter of research and development before World War II. During the war, however, impressive results were achieved (e.g., the development of controlled nuclear fission and penicillin) through major funding commitments. Federal support for the physical sciences waned after the war. Biomedical research through the National Institutes of Health (NIH), however, received increased support throughout the late 1940s and the 1950s. On October 4, 1957, the Soviet Union launched its first Sputnik. Americans were upset by a Soviet-controlled object encircling the Earth and crossing the United States several times a day. Their distress was exacerbated by anti-communist sentiments and suggestions that the Soviet Union had suddenly become technologically superior. The Congress responded by improving appropriations for the National Science Foundation and other grant-making bodies. President Kennedy pledged that the United States would put an astronaut on the moon by 1970. The Great Society programs started by President Johnson in the mid-1960s included the goal of improved social welfare. These commitments resulted in unprecedented increases in federal allocations to academic institutions for research and development. The resulting support did not keep pace with inflation and expansions in the scientific community during the 1970s. Nevertheless, yearly multi-billion dollar appropriations continue to make the federal government the largest supporter of research and development in the United States.

A leveling-off of federal research support in the 1980s, coupled with a shift in national industrial and political priorities, has stimulated increased industrial support of academically based research. This support is likely to become even more important to academic scientists.

Types of Grants

Academicians commonly refer to "grants," but a grant is only one of six instruments for supporting university research and development. These instruments are:

1. Free gift or grant-in-aid
2. Grant
3. Cooperative agreement
4. Contract
5. Fellowship
6. Scholarship

Free Gift or Grant-in-Aid

A grant-in-aid is money that can be spent at the discretion of investigators. No reports to sponsors are necessary for the expenditure of these funds, but it is wise for the investigator to respect the purpose for which the money was given. Grant-in-aid funds are obtained through alumni foundations or fund-raising activities of the faculty. Investigators who do industrially sponsored research have frequent opportunities to solicit free gift funds.

The loose accountability for grant-in-aid funds should not be misconstrued. Investigator discretion has been alluded to, but the ownership of grants should be clearly understood. Nearly all grants are given to institutions, not to individuals. The awards are administered through the institution's accounting office, and an investigator must abide by institutional policy in the expenditure of funds. The greatest "freedom" is afforded to the investigator with a grant-in-aid. The money can be used for salaries and wages, research equipment and supplies, travel to scientific meetings, and office expenses. Moreover, funds can be shifted at the investigator's discretion from one category to another. Free gift money permits maximum flexibility, and that is why this type of funding is the hardest to obtain.

Grant

A grant is a flexible instrument used to support research and scholarly activities. Ideas for grants come from investigators who define the scope of projects.

Granting agencies allow changes in the objective of grants, but accountability is required both in the expenditure of funds and in the conduct of research. Indeed, granting agencies have become more aware in recent years of the need for stated objectives, and they demand evidence of attempts to meet these objectives during the course of the award. This is particularly true for federally sponsored grants.

Cooperative Agreement

A cooperative agreement is similar to a grant, but it provides for more direction by the funding agency during the course of the research. Cooperative agreements have been widely used by the U.S. Department of Agriculture (USDA) and the Environmental Protection Agency (EPA) in recent years.

Contract

A research contract is an agreement to perform carefully defined research. Thus, there is less flexibility in contract research than in grant research. The federal government has funded contracts after receiving unsolicited proposals from investigators. More commonly, federally sponsored contracts are publicized through Request for Proposal (RFP) notices in the *Commerce Business Daily*, and investigators may write for a copy of the RFP.

Jargon used by federal agencies is confusing. The RFP process is no exception. The "actual" RFP requested by the investigator is a document that outlines the objectives of the contract, the criteria for selecting the contractor, and the guidelines for constructing a budget. The latter includes the government's estimate of the number of man-years (equivalent to the number of men and women working full-time for one year) required to fulfill the objectives of the contract. Occasionally RFPs have such specific objectives that they seem to have been written by an investigator already working in the area. This may be a clue that the contract is already activated. Contracts, like grants, come up periodically for competitive renewal, and they will be described in the *Commerce Business Daily*. They can subsequently be bid upon by qualified investigators. An investigator has no way, except by intuition, to know whether the RFP is of the type described. In cases of renewal contracts, unfortunately, the likelihood of the novice attaining funds is slim.

Industrial contracts, like their government counterparts, involve focused research and relatively little freedom to deviate from stated objectives. Industrial firms may be more generous than federal agencies and provide companion grant-in-aid funds. The costs of the contract are negotiated like a business deal. A request for grant-in-aid is articulated as "profit." The "profit" is used to support graduate fellowships and the investigator's personal research.

Grants and contracts are awarded to academic institutions in the name of the investigator. Fellowships and scholarships are often awarded to individuals.

Fellowships and Scholarships

Fellowships provide support for master's, predoctoral, and postdoctoral education and research. Scholarships are awards for undergraduate research and study. Descriptions of federal and private fellowship, scholarship, and grant programs have been published.[25,39,58,68,70] It is worth a few hours' effort to investigate the opportunities available. Also, advisors and department chairmen may know of unique sources of support in a discipline.

Writing Grant Proposals and Applying for Grants

Grantsmanship is the art of obtaining grants. It involves four skills: identifying resources, contacting grant-making institutions, preparing proposals, and applying for grants. These skills are important because an advisor may ask for help to obtain a grant that may be pursued jointly. Department chairmen encourage students to apply for fellowships, which is similar to competing for research grants.

Many departments also require the preparation of an original grant proposal as a part of doctoral candidacy requirements. The proposal may then be defended during an oral examination. This serves two purposes: it helps prepare one for a dissertation oral, and it provides experience necessary for a career in research. Proposal preparation or its equivalent is necessary in academic as well as industrial jobs. Competing for grants is an important part of a scientist's academic life. The industrial scientist may also be involved in efforts to obtain federal grants and contracts. Furthermore, industrial research requires written plans and justifications that are akin to grant proposals.

Writing proposals and applying for grants requires the development of discipline and insights that will help throughout a professional career. Commitment, thoroughness, and patience are essential components of grant-getting. Tolerance of failure is also required, because many proposals are rejected. Overcoming the trauma of rejection is an important lesson for the professional. It also helps researchers cope with failures in their personal lives. I know researchers who have received dozens of grants during their lives. This has meant confronting at least five times that many rejections. Researchers have to develop emotional strength to survive. Survival skills develop with the self-confidence that comes from research accomplishments, and these skills are useful at home as well as at work.

Many books and articles have been written on grantsmanship. It is impossible in the space allotted to thoroughly review the subject. Critical pointers and insights are given below. For a more detailed treatment of grants, the book by White[137] is recommended.

Identifying Resources

Various books[25,39,58,68,70] list sources of grants, contracts, and fellowships. The National Institutes of Health and the National Science Foundation have published guides[93] to their grant programs. Information on foundations is located in directories.[27,48,49,135] The most widely used compilations are produced by The Foundation Center, which is an educational institute chartered through the Board of Regents of New York State. The center maintains national libraries in New York City, Chicago, and Washington, D.C., and it has several regional collections. These libraries or widely available computer data bases (see Table 12) can be used to find information on the more than 3,000 foundations in the United States. One of the data bases described in Table 12 (i.e., GRANTS) is also a source of information on grant programs offered by federal, state, and local governments, and commercial organizations and associations. Besides the names and addresses of foundations, it is important to know the foundations' purposes and activities, assets, numbers and types of grants awarded in recent years, values of low and high grants, fields of application, limitations, and rules for applications. Listings of members of boards of directors should also be sought (see below).

Another agency, the Funding Source Clearinghouse (116 South Michigan Avenue, Chicago, Ill. 60603), will run a search of its records and will designate the 5 to 10 "best prospects" for funding of your research interests. This service may be costly.

Corporate foundations and funds are indexed in several references.[25,27,33,58,68] Industrial contacts made by an advisor may be the best sources of funds.

Contacting Grantors

It is a mistake to prepare a proposal before contacting the granting agency. Federal agencies such as the National Institutes of Health have project officers who are willing to discuss potential proposals. These officials will be optimistic and encouraging even if an idea is not a top priority for their division. They will tell a researcher if an idea is not worth pursuing because of limited funding possibilities.

This is a good place to mention authorized contacts with granting agencies. Generally, universities prohibit application for extramural funding by anyone except faculty-level scientists. Thus, it can be inappropriate for a graduate student to contact a granting agency. Students

Table 12 Data bases available[a] for information on foundations and other granting agencies

Data Base	Description
Foundation Directory	Provides information on >3,000 foundations which have assets of >$1 million and give grants totaling $100,000 annually; from the Foundation Center
Foundation Grants Index	Provides information on grants of >$5,000 awarded by >400 U.S. foundations; from the Foundation Center
National Foundations	Descriptions of >21,000 U.S. foundations which award grants, regardless of the assets of the foundation or the total amounts of grants awarded annually; from the Foundation Directory
GRANTS	Listings of >1,500 grant programs funded by federal, state, and local governments, and by commercial organizations and associations; from Oryx Press

[a] Telephone connection to Lockheed Information System DIALOG.

may be permitted, however, to apply directly for fellowships. An advisor may also enlist the help of graduate students in the early stages of grant seeking.

Foundations and industrial firms should be contacted initially by letter. The inquiry letter to a foundation should be addressed to the person indicated in *The Foundation Directory*,[48] or the Executive Director or Executive Secretary when explicit instructions are not given. The letter should address the following questions:

1. What is to be done?
2. Why is it worth doing?
3. What are the specific objectives?
4. Who is to do the work?
5. What facilities will be required and are they available?
6. How long will the project take?
7. About how much will the project cost?
8. Can a full proposal be submitted?

The last question may be coupled with an offer to visit foundation officials. If you know a member of the board of trustees, he or she may help you get an appointment. Contacts such as these will not compensate for a poor idea or a shoddy proposal. If a proposal is competitive, however, the influence of a board member is invaluable.

Dermer[33] suggests that an atmosphere of friendliness be created during interviews with foundation officials. Officials will be impressed if a researcher is sincere and can explain the proposed research well. The possibility of the foundation funding work as proposed can be explored, but a decision on funding of the project should not be expected. Before the end of the interview, one can ask if a written proposal can be submitted. If so, the official should be given an estimate of when the proposal will be received.

There are no foolproof methods for approaching industrial firms for grant support. A variety of strategies have been suggested that may be useful. The most "primitive" situation occurs when a researcher has a good idea for a project but knows of no one in the industry who may provide guidance to a potential source of funds. This requires developing unsolicited written inquiries that should contain the following:

1. A brief description of the research to be done. This should address some problem that currently exists (e.g., extend claims of a presently marketed product; provide a new source or route to a valuable process).
2. Who will do the work and why they are unusually qualified to perform the needed research. (*Curriculum vitae* should be included in the mailing.)
3. An estimate of how much time will be required for the project and how much it will cost.
4. Facilities and equipment needed to perform the study and whether these are available.
5. A best assessment of the profit potential of the study.
6. The question should be posed — Can a full proposal be submitted?

The choice of potential sources of support should be based on the apparent interests (product lines) of firms. An inquiry should be directed to a scientist or an administrator who is in charge of an appropriate division of the company. Names of logical individuals may be obtained from senior authors of related papers or through one or two judiciously placed phone calls. The industrial firm may request a full proposal. Clear evidence of a lack of interest at this stage or following evaluation of the proposal is usually final and additional follow-ups are futile.

Seeking grant and contract support is like a business venture. There is no substitute for personal contacts with individuals who may expedite requests. Personal interactions at scientific or professional meetings, or with former associates who may be employed in a given firm, are invaluable. Preliminary contacts can be capped by an offer to present a seminar at a company that may have an interest in one's field of study.

Preparing Proposals

Grant proposals are prepared according to guidelines similar to the ones recommended in Chapter 8 for reports and papers. Some granting agencies have their own format that should be adopted. If no format is prescribed (e.g., most foundations and industrial firms), the one below is recommended.

1. Cover page
2. Abstract (with key words underlined)
3. Budget
4. Biographical sketches of investigators
5. Research plan
   a. Specific aims
   b. Significance and background
   c. Pilot studies
   d. Methods
   e. Collaborative assurance
   f. Facilities available
   g. Appendices

The cover page and abstract are developed as indicated for reports (Chapter 8) with two additions. Lines should be included on the cover page for the signatures of the principal investigator and the official who will sign for the university. In the abstract, key words can be underlined for emphasis. The underlining should be limited to 10 words.

The budget includes sums for one or more of the following:

1. Salaries and wages plus fringe benefits
2. Supplies
3. Equipment
4. Computer time
5. Special costs
   a. Maintenance of animals
   b. Patient fees
   c. Rental fees
   d. Analysis
6. Travel
7. Indirect cost
8. Subcontracts

Salaries and wages are set by the university's personnel office. A personnel pay schedule should be available to help plan costs of required positions. Supplies include expendable items such as paper, computer supplies, glassware, and chemicals. Requests for equipment costing more than $1,000 must be carefully justified because most agencies are reluctant to support capital expenditures.

Computer time and special costs for animal maintenance, patient fees, and equipment rental or analysis fees vary from university to university. Telephone calls to appropriate centers on campus should yield fee schedules.

Funding agencies are fussy about paying for travel. Consequently, requests for travel funds should be conservative and justified. The total to this point is called direct cost.

Indirect cost is the surcharge a university assesses to meet basic operating expenses associated with research (e.g., heating, lighting, accounting). It is generally calculated at a percentage of total direct cost or modified total direct cost (i.e., total direct cost minus costs of capital equipment and subcontracts). Subcontracts are developed to fund segments of the research project that can best be done off campus. Rules for implementing subcontracts should be available through a university's sponsored projects office.

Biographical sketches of all investigators should be included in the grant proposal. Each sketch should be no more than two or three pages and should include a list of all publications (with titles) that are relevant to the proposed research. The biographical materials should clearly indicate the relationships of each person to the project.

The research plan should be carefully developed using the writing guidelines noted in Chapter 8. A "talking style" is particularly effective with grant proposals. In the methods section, for example, sentences such as "If this experiment fails to give expected results, we will . . ." give the reviewer an impression of investigator maturity—a blend of optimism and reality.

The aims of the proposal should be clear, focused, and attainable in the project period. Most importantly, they must contain good ideas and hypotheses that embrace problems at the forefront of a field of study.

The significance and background section should include a succinct review of the literature and clear statements about the importance of the work proposed. The background need not include an exhaustive review of the literature. A focused review containing the most important citations is preferable.

The description of pilot studies that led to the proposal can be the most important section of the research plan. Preliminary results support the feasibility of the project and suggest that the total project will not fail. The write-up of pilot work should indicate one's ability to analyze and interpret data, and to test hypotheses. If the pilot results have been good, the chances of getting funds are improved.

The methods section should contain descriptions of the procedures and tests that will be used in the proposed work. Special handling procedures for animals, and safeguards and informed consent procedures for human subjects, should be included. The details should be substantive, but it is not necessary to describe minutiae such as common laboratory operations (e.g., pipetting, solution preparation). It is important to indicate the kinds of data expected (e.g., rates of growth, percent inhibition) and how the data will be analyzed (e.g., t test). The type of data and analytical results that will be necessary to prove hypotheses should also be indicated.

Collaborative arrangements should be described. Who will be responsible for different segments of the study? How are the different investigators uniquely qualified for their tasks? How will the investigators' work be coordinated? Who is responsible for the preparation of reports?

The facilities available for the investigation should be described. Do not include equipment or laboratory facilities that are of remote use. If needed equipment is housed in another department, describe plans for joint use. Cooperative agreements for joint equipment use, as well as collaborative research efforts, should be documented by letters of support. The letters should be collected as appendix material along with preprints of manuscripts, reports, and charts. A letter of support from an influential person such as a congressman or senator should be inserted in the grant proposal before the research plan.

Fellowship applications containing research proposals should be developed as indicated above. Additionally, the fellowship proposal may need a description of courses and research experiences. These details should be organized carefully along with documentation of the support of advisory faculty.

After a proposal is written, it can be judged against criteria commonly used by peer reviewers. Table 13 contains common failings of grant proposals. The major shortcomings are poor ideas, a lack of clarity, thoughtfulness, and organization, and inadequacies of investigators. Dedication and careful preparation are essential to overcome these shortcomings. Critical reviews by an advisor and "writing buddies" will help to refine the work.

Applying for Grants

All agencies have rules for applying for grants including:

- Budgeting guidelines
- Page limitations

Table 13   Common shortcomings of grant proposals[a]

Proposal Section	Problem
Budget	Excessive funds requested
	Capital equipment request unjustified
	Funds requested are insufficient to complete described project
Biographical Sketch and Background of Investigators	Investigator is inexperienced for research
	Insufficient number of investigators
Research Plan	Poorly organized
	Too long
	Poorly written
	Sloppy preparation
Aims	Project scientifically premature – requires more pilot work
	Validity questionable
	Vague or unsound scientifically
	Too ambitious
	Hypotheses poor
Significance and Background	Problem of little significance or repeats previous work
	Assumptions questionable
	Rationale poor
	Literature background poor or inadequate
Pilot Studies	Pilot work ill-conceived
	Data inappropriately analyzed
	Experiments lack imagination
Methods	Methods unsuited to stated objectives
	Unethical or hazardous procedures proposed
	Controls poorly conceived or inadequately described
	Some problems not realized or dealt with properly
	Results will be confusing, difficult to interpret, or meaningless
	Emphasis on data collection rather than interpretation
Collaboration	Cooperative agreement inadequate, vague, or poorly conceived
	No letters of support
Facilities	Equipment lacking, too old, or insufficiently robust for project

[a] Adopted in part from E. M. Allen, Why are research grant applications disapproved? Science **132**:1532–1534, 1960. Reprinted with permission of the publisher, copyright 1960.

- Dates for application
- University-based review
- Preliminary approval before submittal of a proposal
- Number of copies to be submitted

The rules are the mechanics of grantsmanship, and they are important. No matter how worthy an application is, it will not be funded if it is not considered, and it will not be considered unless the rules are followed.

The federal government prepares application forms and booklets for all of its grant and fellowship programs. These materials are available from a sponsored-projects office. The folders will contain details on the application process. RFPs contain similar information on federal contracts. Foundations and industrial firms rarely have written guidelines for grant applications, but certain grant-making societies such as the American Cancer Society and American Heart Association have published rules for grant-seekers.

The published guidelines will address items listed above. Of note are budgetary restrictions. Some programs permit only the funding of stipends. Other programs may allow only material support, or they may have a maximum amount that can be requested. It is wise to adhere closely to such restrictions.

Federal grant application deadlines are coupled to the federal government's fiscal year (October 1 through September 30 of the following year) and to review cycles that occur two or three times a year. The NIH, for example, accepts proposals for new grants on the first of November, March, and July of each year. NIH proposals are subjected to a two-stage review process which has been described by Eaves. [41] The process is completed in nine months.

Deadlines for foundation and industrial grants rarely exist. A grant proposal will be considered at a regularly scheduled meeting by the board of directors of a foundation or by the scientific advisory board of a company. These meetings are convened at regular intervals, and their times are available through the executive officer of a foundation or from a contact person at an industrial firm.

Some foundations require a campus-wide competition prior to the submittal of a proposal. This limits the number of proposals that reach the foundation and saves foundation screening efforts. Personnel in a sponsored projects office should know about such reviews. Internal reviews are also required when research involves animals, human subjects, and biohazards, as indicated in the previous chapter. The appropriate committee chairmen or sponsored-projects office staff can describe procedures used at one's university.

Federal grant and contract programs rarely require approval prior to application. This is not the case with foundations and industrial firms. Researchers waste time if they send unsolicited proposals to these agencies. The pre-proposal inquiries noted earlier are important for foundations and corporations. Proposals should be prepared and sent only after receiving a positive response to inquiry letters.

Unlike publications, a proposal can be submitted to more than one funding agency. The duplication, however, must be dealt with honestly and straightforwardly. The proposal should contain a statement that funds have been sought from more than one agency and that funding by one agency will cause withdrawal of the proposal from all others.

Researchers learn about the fate of their federal grant or contract proposals according to published deadlines in application booklets or RFPs. The review cycle for grants is typically six to nine months. Contract proposals are generally acted upon three months after the submittal deadline. Review periods for foundations and industrial firms vary. It is not unreasonable, however, to make contact with the prospective grantor four to six weeks after submitting a proposal. The telephone conversation could begin with a polite offer to supply more information.

The funding of a grant or fellowship changes one's life. A sense of independence results that bolsters the autonomy needed by scientists. The feeling of self-confidence gained after a satisfactory peer review stimulates new levels of commitment. These psychic boosts help researchers survive the inevitable rejections experienced by all grant seekers.

Successful completion of grant proposals can be an important step toward an advanced degree. The subsequent need to seek a postdoctoral or permanent position is discussed in the next chapter.

Chapter 13

Getting a Job

. . . the hardest work you will ever have to do
is the job of getting a job.
— RICHARD NELSON BOLLES

Career goals are dependent on securing good employment. Obtaining a good job calls for planning and hard work. The job-hunting effort may require the equivalent of three weeks to nine months of full-time effort. The effort is aided by tips on planning, interviewing, and accepting offers.

Planning

Planning should begin early in a graduate career. The planning procedure is guided by the following questions.

- What do I want to do?
- What geographical location is desired?
- How can I secure a position to meet my professional needs and geographical preferences?

The choice of what to do is directed by one's graduate training. It may also be influenced by the job market and career goals. This is particularly true when choosing between a permanent job and a postdoctoral position. Some permanent university positions require postdoctoral experience. A postdoctoral appointment may also be necessary to acquire skills complementary to one's graduate background. Advice should be sought from an advisor and other trusted faculty on the necessity for postdoctoral work in a discipline. It is important, however, to know about the "postdoctoral trap." The researcher who stays in a postdoctoral position for more than two or three years, or one who jumps from

147

one opportunity to another, may have difficulty finding a permanent job. A recent study of the National Research Council[102] reports that ". . . postdoctoral experience is found to contribute little or nothing in terms of subsequent income." Thus, strong lifetime goal-related reasons should exist for choosing the "postdoc route."

A permanent position may be desired in academe, government, or industry. This choice should be based on discussions with faculty and friends located in these environments. An honest self-appraisal of the value placed on creative achievement versus service to others versus financial rewards will help the decision-making process. If one is unsure of choices such as academia or industry, interview opportunities should be sought in both.

Securing an Interview

There are several ways of obtaining an interview for desired employment. These include:

- Personal contacts through an advisor, other faculty, and department chairmen
- Contacts made at professional meetings, including "clearing houses"
- Answering advertisements in professional journals
- Use of executive recruiting firms

Large or prestigious departments are continually informed of employment opportunities through unsolicited mailings from industry, government, and academia. Find out whether notices are posted somewhere in your department. The chairman may have other mechanisms for circulating employment notices to advanced graduate students. Find out what they are, and have your name placed on the routing list.

Contacts at professional meetings are invaluable in developing potential employment opportunities. The widespread use of poster presentations at scientific meetings provides a good mechanism for meeting prospective employers. Because of the importance of these contacts, it is imperative to find a way of participating at one or more professional meetings during a graduate career. These meetings may also have "clearing houses" where employers conduct preliminary interviews with prospective employees. This may require membership in the professional society associated with one's discipline. The "clearing house" service is one of many advantages of joining professional organizations.

Job openings are advertised in professional journals (e.g., *Science*) and specialized publications (e.g., *Chronicle of Higher Education*). Use of the literature throughout one's graduate career will uncover sources. An advisor may also be able to recommend unusual references.

Executive recruiting firms may be used for obtaining leads on industrial positions. Recommendations of firms may be obtained from an advisor or friends in industry. Lists of executive recruiting firms have also been published.[37,99]

Before engaging a recruiting firm, ask for the names and telephone numbers of at least three people who have used their services. Call these people and ask them to relate their experiences with the firm. More than one executive recruiting firm may be engaged; however, for the sake of logistics, I recommend enlisting no more than three. Never allow recruiters to handle your employment exclusively even if they ask.

Develop an understanding immediately with the executive recruiter that a curriculum vitae (CV) is to be sent out only after you have given permission. Some recruiters blanket employers with CVs in an attempt to establish priority on contacts you may have made yourself. Keep notes on all telephone conversations with recruiters. Map the progress of employment contacts. Have your notes handy when calls are made.

Bolles[14] notes that executive recruiters possibly handle as many as 50 percent of professional positions with annual salaries above $15,000. In practically all cases fees are paid by employers; however, be sure to check. If a fee is asked for, go elsewhere.

Many universities have placement bureaus. These are of limited usefulness to graduates with advanced degrees. The bureaus may, however, serve as a clearinghouse for letters of reference. For a nominal fee, the bureaus will send letters of recommendations to as many prospective employers as designated by you. This minimizes going back to references for letters of recommendation. A bureau's letter-handling service may also be of value when changing jobs in the future.

Postdoctoral positions are frequently offered and accepted without an interview. This is neither good for the offerer nor you. If at all possible, seek an interview even if it is at your expense. A year or two of study under an incompatible advisor can be catastrophic. The guidelines elaborated previously (Chapter 3) can be used when choosing a prospective postdoctoral advisor.

Requests for Interviews

Interview requests are made indirectly through inquiry letters. A letter is sent in response to a personal contact or advertisement, or as unsolicited correspondence. Inquiry letters may have to be sent in great numbers, sometimes as many as hundreds. Success with this effort, like that of a career, is dependent on the strength of applicants' credentials and their persistence. Excellent students find good positions regardless of economic conditions. Mediocre students always have difficulties, and they may encounter many disappointments during recessions.

An inquiry letter should express interest in the opening and the organization or institution. Make reference to specific contacts or announcements. Tailor the correspondence to the particular situation. Never send a form letter or one that is handwritten.

Include a CV in the inquiry correspondence. The CV may be customized for the position; guides for preparing résumés are available.[12,66,74] In general, the CV should contain some personal data including one's social security number, which is often necessary to process interview expense reimbursement checks. Also include telephone numbers where you can be reached during the day and in the evening. Outline your education, research and teaching (when relevant) skills, and honors received. List your publications, including titles, and give names of three or four professionals who are familiar with your talents. Be sure to have permission to cite these references. Offer to have letters of recommendations forwarded and to supply additional information if needed. The inquiry correspondence should be grammatically correct, free from misspellings, and reflective of your personality. Before sending out the first one, ask for a review by an advisor and a couple of close friends.

Initial correspondence can be followed by a letter or a telephone call after a few weeks have elapsed. Sometimes things get bogged down at the employer's end and the reminder is useful. It is often true, however, that applications from highly desirable candidates are acted upon quickly, and the longer the wait, the less the chances are of receiving a positive response.

Another way to follow-up an application is to contact friends or acquaintances at the applicant organization. Don't ask friends to give inside appraisals. These sources, however, can often indicate whether the application is moving along and when you are likely to hear something official. This quells anxieties.

In a perfect world, prompt acknowledgments of all correspondence would be received and quick decisions would be made on requests for consideration. Unfortunately, neither happens often. Additionally, one must become prepared for rejection shock. After receiving a number of turn-downs applicants' self-esteem may erode to the point where they suspect that there is something wrong with them. Bolles[14] suggests that this can lead to lower expectations, depression, desperation, and apathy. Don't let it happen. I have witnessed the placement of hundreds of students in academia and industry. Success goes to those who have dogged determination and those who are willing to expend extraordinary effort in the job-hunting process.

Invitation to Interview

Interview invitations are frequently extended during telephone calls. Become mentally and physically prepared for this possibility. Have an appointment calendar handy to anticipate discussions of times for the interview. Be flexible. Try to accommodate the employer. If given a choice of dates, plan to arrive on a Sunday. This allows time for exploration before the interview and is particularly helpful if the employer is in a large and unfamiliar city. Be sure you understand permissible expenses before traveling. A prospective employer may not be willing to reimburse expenses for certain items (e.g., rental cars).

Preparing for Interviews

Make a folder for each interview. Include in it questions about the opening as well as personal information needed (e.g., housing costs, schools for children). As the interview progresses, take notes which will help answer the questions in writing during free moments. Use the unanswered questions as reminders for additional inquiries.

When possible, make a list of employees that you are likely to meet during an interview. For example, a chemical engineering major interviewing for a faculty position at the University of Rochester could obtain a faculty departmental roster through the Directory of Graduate Research.[38] Similar directories are available in many academic fields. Industrial positions may make it more difficult to locate prospective colleagues; however, some judicious phone calls and the use of directories from professional societies may provide leads to individuals who will be met during the interview.

Once a list is compiled, obtain biographical information on each individual. Of particular importance are research and scholarly interests. Few things are more impressive to prospective employers than interviewees who are able to anticipate interests and concerns of the employer's institution. If possible, try to determine the organizational structure of the interviewing unit. Make a chart of this structure as it is understood. Later, questions can be asked about the organization and errors corrected.

Prepare a short historical and geographical profile on the location of the interview site. Encyclopedic sources and information obtained from a chamber of commerce will be sufficient. This profile serves two purposes. It will make the trip more enjoyable, and it will provide conversation material for less technically skilled people (including upper management) that may be met socially during the interview.

Anticipate questions that may arise during the interview. For example:

- Why do you want this job?
- How are you uniquely qualified?
- What would you like to be doing five years from now? (Be careful of this one. If the interviewer's job is described through your answer, you may appear to be a threat.)
- What activities do you like the most? Like least? Why?
- How can you help our organization?

Be sure to understand what will be required during the interview. Many organizations request that a seminar be given on graduate research work. If one is interviewing for an academic post, a more elementary presentation may also be required to test potential teaching skills. Some universities provide a service involving videotaping of a lecture given at home. The resulting videotape is sent to prospective interviewers for preliminary viewing. I am not aware of anyone who has evaluated the pitfalls of such a practice.

Never ask to bring a spouse on an initial interview. The question is presumptuous and should be saved for subsequent contacts.

Be aware of prospective employers' possible biases about personal appearance. Neatness and conservative dress are recommended for industrial interviews. It may surprise you to learn that it is still common in some firms to see only white shirts worn by male employees. Business suits are recommended for women and men.

University faculty are generally tolerant of different dress styles. Nevertheless, jackets and ties are recommended for men and equivalent dress for women interviewing in academia.

The Interview

Job interviews give researchers and their prospective employers opportunities to evaluate each other. Interviews provide chances to convince employers that your skills and personality meet their needs. You can influence the decision-making process by preparations before the interviews and your performance during them.

Be sure you know who the interview contact person is and who will meet you at the airport. Soon after this meeting, ask for a copy of the itinerary for the interview and clarify apparent ambiguities with the contact person. Begin memorizing the names of the contact person and people you are scheduled to meet. It is important to remember at least first names as the interview proceeds.

Be sure to be on time for all meetings during the interview. Continually show interest in the interviewers — their research, problems, and concerns. Ask questions from your interview folder, making sure to avoid those that can be answered by reading materials that may have been received as a part of the interview. Also, be sure to learn what is expected of the person filling the job that is open and what benefits accrue. It is inappropriate to discuss salary unless an interviewer takes the initiative. It is wise, however, to have a minimum salary level in mind to anticipate a relevant question from the prospective employer.

The characteristics of a good scientific presentation have already been covered in Chapter 10. Some elements, however, are unique to interviews. The audience may be a mixture of scientists, managers, and administrators. Pitch the talk accordingly. Speak clearly and at a moderate pace. Be sure to communicate enthusiasm for your work. If one is not enthusiastic now, how can prospective employers expect enthusiasm for work vital to their institutions? Point out potentialities for additional investigations that were uncovered through your research. This highlights creative abilities. Incorporate into the talk some of your philosophy and approaches to research. Keep the presentation to 50 minutes. Repeat questions so all can hear them and answer each question directly. If you are stumped, say so. Honesty at this stage and throughout the interview is imperative.

During an interview, you will meet with your prospective supervisor one or more times. For an academic appointment, you will want to know:

- What rank is assigned to the position — instructor or assistant professor?
- Is the position a tenure-track one? What are the guidelines for promotion to associate professor? For tenure?
- Is the position a 9- or 12-month one? If 9 month, is there potential for summer teaching salary?
- Is it a hard or soft money position? (Hard money positions are funded through line-items in the regular departmental budget. At a state university, hard money lines are funded by the legislature. Soft money lines are dependent on grants or other temporary sources of funding.)
- What are typical teaching loads? Are there special accommodations during the first year to help you to establish a research program? How are team-taught courses handled?
- What start-up funds are available for research? (In the physical, chemical, or biological sciences, it is not uncommon to request $25,000 to $100,000 in start-up research funds, principally for major equipment.)
- What other resources are available? Seed grants? Technical help?

Secretarial support? Other support services such as libraries, computer center, animal resources, photoservices? Travel support?

- What office and laboratory spaces would be made available to you? Ask to see these areas.
- What are the fringe benefits: insurance plans, retirement including personal and university contributions, medical–dental–optical care, social security contribution, education benefits for you or your family, recreational and cultural offerings?
- What types of committee and continuing education (if relevant) assignments are common?
- What are the future growth and development plans for the department? For the university?

If an industrial position is being sought the following additional questions are relevant.

- Are there savings and stock option plans? How do they work?
- Will the company pay moving expenses? What about househunting trips with a spouse?

With government positions, explore the Government Service (GS) rules and how they pertain to you. Throughout this question and answer portion of the interview, express empathy for the employer's position and try not to make your questions sound like a litany of selfish appeals.

After returning from the interview, send short thank you notes to people who were kind to you during the visit. Be sure to ask who receives expense reimbursement requests and what types of receipts are required.

The Offer

Initial offers are frequently made over the phone. No offer is firm, however, until it has been received in writing. The written offer should include the following:

- Rank
- Expected starting date
- Salary
- Description of financial remuneration for moving
- Contingencies (e.g., offer contingent on receipt of Ph.D.)
- Materials describing fringe benefits

Seek an advisor's assessment of the merits of the offer. Try to answer written offers promptly. Ten days to two weeks is a reasonable time to make a decision. Stalling for more time can be detrimental.

With luck, two or more offers may be received to choose from. The acceptance letter is easy to write—the rejection one difficult. Remember that a rejection letter is difficult for an employer to receive after he or she has spent considerable effort to interview you. Be sure to refer to the assets of his or her institution and allude to any difficulty you had in making a decision. You and this employer are colleagues, and you are likely to interact again in the future.

You should expect to find a good position. Your career will be rewarding. I leave you with these optimistic prospects. Journey back through these pages as needed. *Bonne chance* and *bon voyage*!

Appendix 1

Data Bases Available* for Searches of the Scientific Literature

Data Base	Description	Years of Coverage
AGRICOLA	Worldwide journal and monograph literature on agriculture and related subjects, from the National Agricultural Library	1970–
AQUACULTURE	Growth requirements, engineering, and economics of marine, brackish, and freshwater organisms; from National Oceanic and Atmospheric Administration	1970–
AQUALINE	Abstracts from world literature on water, waste water, and aquatic environments; from Water Research Centre, Stevenage, U.K.	1974–
ASFA (Aquatic Sciences and Fisheries Abstracts)	Life sciences of seas and inland waterways plus legal, political, and social implications of aquatic life; from UNESCO	1978–
BIOSIS Previews	International coverage of life science research; from *Biological Abstracts*	1969–
CA Search	International coverage of chemical sciences; from Chemical Abstracts Service	1967–
CLAIMS/CHEM	U.S. patents of chemically related products and processes with some foreign equivalents; from IFI/Plenum Data Co.	1950–1970
CLAIMS/CHEM/ UNITERM	Similar to CLAIMS/CHEM but with special subject indexing and easier retrieval of information; from IFI/ Plenum Data Co.	1950–

* Telephone connection to Lockheed Information System DIALOG, System Development Corporation's ORBIT, and Bibliographic Retrieval Service, Inc.

Data Base	Description	Years of Coverage
CLAIMS/U.S. Patent Abstracts	Abstracts and citations for U.S. patents in aerospace and aeronautical engineering, chemical engineering, chemistry, civil engineering, electrical and electronic engineering, electromagnetic technology, mechanical engineering, nuclear science, and general science and technology; from IFI/Plenum Data Co.	1978–
COMPENDEX	International coverage of engineering sciences; from Engineering Index, Inc.	1970–
Comprehensive Dissertation Abstracts	Author, title and subject guide to nearly all American dissertations since 1861 and many from foreign countries; abstracts added beginning in July 1981; from Xerox University Microfilms	1861–
Conference Papers Index	Records of scientific and technical papers presented at major regional, national, and international meetings each year; Data Courier, Inc.	1973–
CRIS (Current Research Information System)	Research in agricultural sciences; U.S. Department of Agriculture State Research Service	July 1974–
Electronics and Computers	Worldwide coverage of literature in: electronic physics, circuits and devices; communications; computer software, applications, mathematics, and electronics; from Cambridge Scientific Abstracts	1978–
Energyline	Energy issues and problems; from Environment Information Center, Inc.	1971–
Enviroline	International coverage of: biology, chemistry, economics, geology, law, management, planning, political science, and technology of environmental issues; from Environment Information Center, Inc.	1971–
Environmental Bibliography	Atmospheric studies, energy, general human ecology, land resources, nutrition and health, and water resources; Environmental Studies Institute	1973–
Excerpta Medica	Worldwide citations and abstracts from 3,500 biomedical journals; from *Excerpta Medica*	1974–

Data Base	Description	Years of Coverage
GEOARCHIVE	International coverage of geological sciences; from Geosystems	1969–
GEOREF	Coverage of >3,000 journals in geosciences including conferences and major symposia; from the American Geological Institute	1967–
INSPEC	Coverage of literature in computers, electrotechnology, and physics; from the American Institute of Electrical Engineers	1969–
IPA (*International Pharmaceutical Abstracts*)	Literature on drug development and use of drugs; from the American Society of Hospital Pharmacy	1970–
IRL Life Sciences Collection	Worldwide coverage of life sciences including conferences; from Information Retrieval Ltd.	1978–
ISI/BIOMED	Index of >1,400 biomedical journals; from the Institute of Scientific Information	1979–
ISI/COMPUMATH	Covers literature in computer science, mathematics, statistics, operations research, and related areas; from the Institute for Scientific Information	1976–
ISI/GEOSCITEC	Covers literature in geosciences, petroleum science, oceanography, marine technology, metallurgy, mining, mineralogy, meteorology, atmospheric science, and related fields. Approximately 350 journals fully indexed; 6,300 other journals selectively indexed; from the Institute for Scientific Information	1978–
ISI/ISTP&B	Computerized version of Scientific and Technical Proceedings and Books. Covers >3,000 proceedings and >1,500 books annually; from the Institute for Scientific Information	1978–
LISA (*Library and Science Abstracts*)	International coverage of library and information science literature; from Learned Information, Ltd.	1969–
MEDLINE	Citations from *Index Medicus, International Nursing Index*, and *Index to Dental Literature*; from the National Library of Medicine	1966–

Data Base	Description	Years of Coverage
METADEX (*Metals Abstracts/Alloys Index*)	International coverage of metallurgical sciences literature; from the American Society of Metals and Metals Society of London	1966–
Microcomputer Index	Subject and abstract guide to 21 microcomputer journals; from Microcomputer Information Services	1981–
NIMH	Mental health literature from >950 journals, symposia, government reports and other sources; from the National Institute of Mental Health	1969–
Non-ferrous Metals Abstracts	Non-ferrous metallurgical science and technology; from the British Non-Ferrous Metals Technology Centre	1961–
Oceanic Abstracts	International literature on: geology, governmental and legal aspects of marine resources, marine biology, marine pollution, meteorology, and oceanography; from Data Courier, Inc.	1964–
Pollution Abstracts	Literature on environmental pollution, its sources, and its control; from Data Courier, Inc.	1970–
Population Bibliography	International coverage of population research: abortion, demography, family planning, fertility studies, and migration; from Carolina Population Center, University of North Carolina	1966–
PRE-MED	Weekly updated citations from 125 of the most current important biomedical journals that make up the *Abridged Index Medicus*; from the National Library of Medicine	
Psychological Abstracts	Worldwide coverage of literature in psychology and related social–behavioral literature; from the American Psychological Association	1967–
Safety Science	Literature on environmental and industrial safety; from Cambridge Scientific Abstracts, Inc.	1975–
SCISEARCH	International literature of sciences and technology; from the Institute for Scientific Information	1974–

Data Base	Description	Years of Coverage
SOCIAL SCISEARCH	Worldwide coverage of social and behavioral sciences literature; from the Institute for Scientific Information	1972–
Sociological Abstracts	International coverage of literature in sociology and related social–behavioral sciences; from Sociological Abstracts, Inc.	1963–
SPIN	Literature published by the American Institute of Physics on: astronomy, astrophysics, geophysics, mathematical and statistical physics; from the American Institute of Physics	1975–
SSIE Current Research (Smithsonian Science Information Exchange)	Reports from private and governmentally sponsored research projects initiated or completed during past two years; from the Smithsonian Institution	Past two years
TELEGEN	Covers literature on biotechnology and genetic engineering in >7,000 sources including conference and symposia papers, government studies, periodicals, and the popular press; from Environment Information Center, Inc.	1973–
Zoological Record	Covers zoological literature from >6,000 journals; from BioSciences Information Service and the Zoological Society of London	1978–

Appendix 2

Examples of Jargon and Preferred Words and Expressions*

Jargon	Preferred Word or Expression
a majority of; the great majority of	most
a number of	many
absolutely complete	complete
accounted for by the fact; due to the fact that; on account; as a consequence of; based on the fact that	because
adequate enough	adequate
along the lines of	like
analyzation	analysis
an example of this is the fact that	today
as to whether	whether
at an earlier date	previously
attached together	attached
at the present time; at this point in time	now
basic fundamentals	fundamentals
beg to differ	disagree
definitely proved	proved
disappear from sight	disappear
due to the fact that	due to
during the year of 1983	during 1983
enclosed herein	enclosed
end result	result
exactly identical	identical
exhibit a tendency to	tend to
few (many) in number	few (many)
finalize	end

*From R. A. Day, How to write and publish a scientific paper, 2nd ed., ISI Press, Philadelphia, 1983, and D. W. Ewing, Writing for results in business, government, and the professions, Wiley, New York, 1974. Reprinted by permission of the publishers.

Jargon	Preferred Word or Expression
following after	after
for the purpose of	for
has the capability of	can
have at hand	have
hold in abeyance	wait
in accordance with your request	as you requested
in a number of cases	some
in close proximity	close, near
in order to	to
in some cases	sometimes
institute an improvement	improve
in a matter of	about
in the not-too-distant future	soon
in the normal course	normally
in the proximity of	near
in the same way as described	as described
in the state of Delaware	in Delaware
in view of	because, since
involve the necessity of	require
it has been brought to my attention	I have learned
it has been reported by Smith	Smith reported
it is incumbent on me	I must
it is often the case that	often
it is suggested that; it may be that	I think
it is worth pointing out in this context that	note that
it may, however, be noted that	but
it would not be unreasonable	I (we) assume
join together	join
joint cooperation	cooperation
kindly return same	please return
make an approximation of	estimate
make mention of	mention
make the acquaintance of	meet
melt down	melt
merge together	merge
minimize as far as possible	minimize
modern methods of today	modern methods
more preferable	preferable
mutual cooperation	cooperation
my personal opinion	my opinion
on account of the conditions described	because of these conditions
permit me to take this opportunity	I want to
perform an analysis of	analyze
plan ahead	plan
potential opportunity	opportunity

Jargon	Preferred Word or Expression
pursuant to your request	as you requested
report back	report
repeat the same step	repeat the step
single unit	unit
state the point that	state that
still continue	continue
still remain	remain
surrounding circumstances	circumstances
take cognizance of	note
thank you kindly	thank you
this is to acknowledge receipt of	thank you for
this result would seem to indicate	this result indicates
through the use of	by; with
to be cognizant of	to know; to understand
to summarize the above	in summary
total effect of	effect of
to the fullest possible extent	fully
true facts	facts
ultimate	last
ultimate end	end
utilize	use
very unique	unique
was of the opinion that	believed
we wish to thank	we thank
within the realm of possibility	possible
with reference to	concerning
with the possible exception of	exception
with the result that	so that

Appendix 3

Guidelines for the Preparation of Consent Forms for Human Subjects Research

The consent form should be a statement addressed to the subject and should read as such. Ordinarily, it is best worded in the second person. It must be in language the subject can understand. This includes avoiding or defining technical terminology, adjusting for educational background, and providing translations into other languages when members of the anticipated subject population do not understand English.

The checklist of points to be covered in the written consent form applies to all kinds of research although some points may not apply to every study. The checklist is numbered, but these numbers should not appear on the consent form. The consent form should include the following:

1. A STATEMENT OF THE GENERAL PURPOSE OF THE STUDY
2. AN INVITATION TO PARTICIPATE
   Points 1 and 2 can be combined in languages such as, "You are invited to participate in a study of . . . We hope to learn . . ." Such an invitation helps to communicate that there is a choice to be made.
3. WHY THIS SUBJECT WAS SELECTED AND HOW MANY SUBJECTS ARE INVOLVED
   Example: Selection is because he is a normal adult male, has asthma, or has relatives with a specific disease. This inclusion of subject criteria helps the subject assess the nature and importance of participation. If the statement of the purpose of the study identifies the subject population, it need not be repeated here. State approximately how many subjects there will be in the study.
4. THE PROCEDURES TO BE FOLLOWED
   This statement should include a description of the procedures, how long they will take, and their frequency. Use of randomization or placebos should be disclosed. If any of the procedures are experimental, they should be identified as such.
5. DISCOMFORTS AND INCONVENIENCES
   Describe the discomforts and inconveniences that might reasonably be ex-

164

pected. For example, many studies use venipuncture to obtain blood specimens from subjects. A statement such as the following can be used to explain venipuncture to the prospective subject: "Venipuncture is a method of obtaining blood samples by inserting a needle into a vein in the arm and withdrawing a sample of blood. It is a routine procedure used to remove blood specimens from patients as well as healthy persons undergoing physical examinations. Venipuncture is accompanied by minor discomfort at the site of needle entry and may result in slight bruising at this site." An estimate of the total amount of the subject's time required must be included if it is not clear from the procedure description.

6. IF THERE ARE ANY RISKS IN INVOLVEMENT, A DESCRIPTION OF THEM

A subject at risk means any individual who may be exposed to the possibility of physical, psychological or social injury, as a consequence of participation as a subject in any research, development, or related activity which departs from the activities necessary to meet his or her needs. It also pertains to increases in the ordinary risks of daily life, including the recognized risks inherent in a chosen occupation or field of service. When appropriate, a statement should appear in the consent form that a procedure may involve unforeseeable risks.

7. IF ANY BENEFITS TO THE SUBJECT CAN REASONABLY BE EXPECTED, A DESCRIPTION OF THEM

The suggestion of a benefit can be a strong inducement to participation. Thus, it should be limited to substantial and likely benefits. If the benefits to control subjects are different from the benefits to other subjects, this should be made clear. State that significant findings will be supplied to the subject (if they are relevant to the subject's health or well-being.)

8. TREATMENT OF PHYSICAL INJURY RESULTING FROM RESEARCH

Subjects must be informed of the provision made for injury that may result from their participation in research. In cases where emergency medical attention for research-related injuries is arranged, a disclaimer for extended care should be put into the consent form, such as "continuing medical care and/or hospitalization for research-related injury will not be provided free of charge nor will financial compensation be available." If no provision has been made for treatment of research-related injuries then this should be stated.

9. STANDARD TREATMENT WITHHELD OR ALTERNATIVE PROCEDURES AVAILABLE

If any standard treatment is being withheld, it should be disclosed. If there are any other appropriate alternative procedures that might be advantageous to the subject, describe them. "Appropriate" and "advantageous" should be interpreted in terms of the spectrum of responsible professional judgment, not by the investigator's personal judgment alone. If the alternative therapies are too numerous to specify, a statement such as "Alternative procedures which would be potentially advantageous have been described" could be included in the consent form rather than going into elaborate detail.

10. CONFIDENTIALITY

If data obtained will be made available to any person or organization other than the subject, the investigator, and the investigator's staff, the person or agencies to whom information will be furnished, the purpose of the disclosure, and the nature of the information to be furnished must be described.

Data in the form of tape recordings, photographs, movies, or videotapes require special attention. If they are to be made, they should be described even if they will not be shown to others.

Use of such data for other purposes must be disclosed and permission obtained in a special portion of the consent form. Final disposition of any such data should also be included.

11. COMPENSATION AND COSTS

If the subject will receive payment, the amount must be described or stated. If subjects receive services or treatment at a lower cost than would be charged non-subjects, the reduction in cost is a form of compensation for participation. If there might be additional cost to the subject resulting from participation, this must be disclosed. Prorated payments when applicable should be described.

12. AN INDICATION THAT THE SUBJECT IS FREE TO DECIDE NOT TO PARTICIPATE OR LATER TO WITHDRAW CONSENT AND DISCONTINUE PARTICIPATION WITHOUT PREJUDICE

This section must not contain any exculpatory language (e.g., before you withdraw you must inform the investigator). An example of a satisfactory inclusion is, "Your decision whether or not to participate will not prejudice your present or future association (treatment, if applicable) with (indicate name of institution or individual). If you decide to participate, you are free to discontinue participation at any time without prejudice." State conditions (if relevant) under which the subject's participation would be discontinued by the investigator. Also, describe consequences of a subject withdrawal from participation. This is particularly relevant if participation in the research involves treatment of a health-related problem and withdrawal would adversely affect that treatment.

13. AN OFFER TO ANSWER QUESTIONS

Include the name, phone number, and address of an investigator that the subject can contact if he or she has further questions, and state that this information is for that purpose.

14. A STATEMENT THAT THE SUBJECT WILL BE OFFERED A COPY OF THE CONSENT FORM

In all situations employing a signed, written consent document, the investigator must offer each subject or her or his representative a copy of the consent form. The reasons for this are as follows: First, it helps the subject to maintain continuing understanding of her or his involvement in the research and can help to avoid problems should the subject forget that he or she has been informed previously of a risk or discomfort. Second, giving the subject a copy of the consent form helps the subject to recognize differences between his or her actual experience and what was expected. Finally, this contributes to preserving a good relationship between the investigator and subject.

15. AGREEMENT TO PARTICIPATE

There are several approaches to the language expressing the subject's decision to participate; for example, "You are making a decision whether or not to participate. Your signature indicates that, having read the information provided above, you have decided to participate and understand that you have the right to withdraw at any time without prejudice." If someone other than the subject is giving consent (e.g., parents; in cases of research with individuals less than 18 years old the signature of only one parent is ordinarily required), the suggested language should be changed to: "You are making a decision regarding participation. Your signature indicates that you have read the above information and you have decided to permit (subject's name) to participate." Children who are capable of some understanding should be given an opportunity to refuse to participate. The best way to document that the child has been given this opportunity is to obtain the child's written consent, though this is of doubtful legal value. Alternatively, assent may be documented through a simple statement, "(name) provided verbal assent before this investigator on (date)" which subsequently should be signed by the investigator. In cases where surveys or related instruments are used, a maximum of two follow-ups are prudently employed to improve return rates. This limitation is advised to avoid harassment or feelings of coercion.

16. SIGNATURES

There must be space for signatures and for the date of signature. If applicable, there should be space for the signature of one other person (e.g., parent, guardian), along with a space for the signer to indicate his or her relationship to the subject. The signature of the investigator is recommended in order that it can be established who discussed the study with the subject. If applicable, there should be space for a signature of a witness.

SAMPLE CONSENT FORM

You are invited to participate in a study of (state what is being studied). We hope to learn (state what the study is designed to discover or establish). You were selected as a possible participant in this study because (state why the subject was selected). There will be (number) subjects in the study.

If you decide to participate, we (or: Dr. _____ and his associates) will (Describe the procedures to be followed, including their purposes, how long they will take, and their frequency. Describe the discomforts and inconveniences reasonably to be expected, and estimate the total time required. Describe the risks reasonably to be expected, and any benefits reasonably to be expected).

(Describe appropriate alternative procedures that might be advantageous to the subject, if any. Any standard treatment that is being withheld must be disclosed).

Any information that is obtained in connection with this study and that can be identified with you will remain confidential and will be disclosed only with your permission. (If you will be releasing information to anyone for any reason, you must state the persons or agencies to whom the information will be furnished, the nature of the information to be furnished, and the purpose of the disclosure).

Your decision whether or not to participate will not prejudice your future relations with the (Institution or agency). If you decide to participate, you are free to discontinue participation at any time without prejudice.

If you have any questions, please ask us. If you have any additional questions later, Dr. _____ (give a phone number or address) will be happy to answer them. You will be offered a copy of this form to keep.

You are making a decision whether or not to participate. Your signature indicates that you have read the information provided above and have decided to participate. You may withdraw at any time without prejudice after signing this form should you choose to discontinue participation in this study.

_____   _____

Signature   Date

_____   _____

(Signature of Parent or Legal Guardian)   Date

(This line should not appear on forms that will be given to subjects consenting for themselves.)

_____   _____

Signature of Witness (when appropriate)   Signature of Investigator

References

1. AAUP Directory. 1982–83. The Association of American University Presses, New York.
2. Abelson, P. H. 1982. Excessive zeal to publish. Science **218**:953.
3. Albert, A. 1960. Selective toxicity, 2nd ed. Wiley, New York.
4. American National Standards Institute, Inc. 1969. American national standard for writing abstracts. ANSI Z39.5-1969. American National Standards Institute, Inc., New York.
5. Audio courses catalogue. 1982. American Chemical Society, Washington, D.C.
6. Austin, J. H. 1978. Chase, chance, and creativity. Columbia University Press, New York.
7. Bauer, E. J. 1977. The "KISS" principle for speaker slide preparation: keep it simple stupid! Med. Meet. **4**(3):32.
8. Beecher, H. K. 1966. Ethics and clinical research. New Engl. J. Med. **274**:1354–1360.
9. Belmont Report. 1979. Ethical principles and guidelines for the protection of human subjects of research; report of the National Commission for the Protection of Human Subjects of Biomedical and Behavioral Research. Fed. Register **44**(76):23192–23197, April 18.
10. Beveridge, W. I. 1957. The art of scientific investigation. Revised ed. Norton, New York.
11. Bibliographic guide to government publications – U.S. 1978. Vols. 1 and 2. Hall, Boston.
12. Biegeleisen, J. I. 1976. Job resumes: How to write them, how to present them, preparing for interviews. Grosset and Dunlap, New York.
13. Bogardus, E. S. 1934. Leaders and leadership. Appleton-Century, New York.
14. Bolles, R. N. 1980. What color is your parachute? A practical manual for job-hunters and career changers. Ten Speed Press, Berkeley, Calif.
15. Books in print. 1982. Author Vols. 1–3, Titles Vols. 4–6. Bowker, New York.
16. Booth, V. 1981. Writing a scientific paper and speaking at scientific meetings. The Biochemical Society, London.
17. Brady, J. V. 1978. Workshop on Institutional Procedures for the Protection of Human Subjects, Organized by the Division of Scientific Investigations, Bureau of Drugs, U.S. Food and Drug Administration, New Orleans.
18. Brady, J. V., and A. R. Jonsen. 1982. The evolution of regulatory influences on research with human subjects. *In* R. A. Greenwald, M. K. Ryan, and J. E.

Mulvihill (eds.), Human Subjects Research, pp. 3–18. Plenum Press, New York.

19. Brown, H. C. 1981. Adventures in research. Chem. Eng. News **59**(14):24–29.
20. Calvert, J. G., J. N. Pitts, Jr., and G. H. Dorion. 1972. Graduate school in the sciences: entrance, survival, and careers. Wiley-Interscience, New York.
21. Casey, R. S., and J. W. Perry. 1951. Punched cards—their application to science and industry. Reinhold, New York.
22. Classification of etiologic agents on the basis of hazard. 1974. 4th ed. DHEW, Public Health Service, Center for Disease Control, Office of Biosafety, Atlanta, Ga.
23. Code of Federal Regulations, Title **9**—Animals and Animal Products, Publication No. 340-938/APHIS-4268. 1980. U.S. Government Printing Office, Washington, D.C.
24. Code of Federal Regulations, 45 CFR 46. 1983. Title **45**—Public Welfare. Publication No. 0-406-756. Protection of Human Subjects. Revised as of March 8, 1983. U.S. Government Printing Office, Washington, D.C.
25. The complete grants sourcebook for higher education. 1980. American Council on Education, Washington, D.C.
26. Cook, M. G. 1975. The new library key, 3rd ed. Wilson, New York.
27. The corporate fund raising directory. 1982. 1983–1984 ed. Public Services Materials Center, New York.
28. Corwin, A. H. 1977. Proceedings of the Robert A. Welch Conferences on Chemical Research. XX. American chemistry bicentennial. W. O. Milligan (ed.), pp. 45–69. Robert A. Welch Foundation, Houston, Tex.
29. Davis, E. B. 1981. Using the biological literature: a practical guide. Dekker, New York.
30. Day, R. A. 1983. How to write and publish a scientific paper, 2nd ed. ISI Press, Philadelphia.
31. DEA registration information. 1984. Drug Enforcement Administration Booklet Containing 21 CFR, Part 1300 to 1316.81. U.S. Government Printing Office, Washington, D.C.
32. Deichmann, W. B., and H. W. Gerarde. 1969. Toxicology of drugs and chemicals, 4th ed. Academic Press, New York.
33. Dermer, J. 1975. How to raise funds from foundations; Dermer, J., and S. Wertheimer. 1982. The complete guide to corporate fund raising. Public Service Materials Center, New York.
34. Design criteria for viral oncology research facilities. 1975. DHEW Publication No. (NIH) 76-891. U.S. Government Printing Office, Washington, D.C.
35. Dictionary of science & technology. 1979. A. F. Dorian (ed.). Elsevier, New York.
36. Dictionary of scientific and technical terms. 1974. 2nd ed. D. N. Lapedes (ed.), McGraw-Hill, New York.
37. Directory of executive recruiters. 1983. 14th ed. Consultant News, Fitzwilliam, N.H.
38. Directory of graduate research. 1983. American Chemical Society, Washington, D.C.
39. Directory of research grants. 1982. W. K. Wilson and B. K. Wilson (eds.). Oryx, Pheonix, Ariz.

40. Dreisbach, R. H. 1983. Handbook of poisoning, 11th ed. Lange Medical Publications, Los Altos, Calif.

41. Eaves, G. N. 1972. Who reads your project-grant application to the National Institutes of Health? Fed. Proc. **31**:2–9.

42. Educational film locator. 1980. 2nd ed. Bowker, New York.

43. Educators guide to free audio and video materials. 1981. 28th ed. W. A. Wittich (ed.). Educators Progress Service, Randolph, Wisc.

44. Ewing, D. W. 1974. Writing for results in business, government, and the professions. Wiley, New York.

45. Federal guidelines for research involving recombinant DNA molecules. 1982. Fed. Regist. **47**(167):38048–38068, August 27.

46. F.A.S. (Federation of American Scientists) Public Interest Report. 1977. **30**(8):8.

47. Fielden, J. 1966. "What do you mean I can't write?" Harvard Bus. Rev., May–June, pp. 144–156.

48. The foundation directory. 1979. 7th ed. M. O. Lewis (ed.). The Foundation Center, New York; The foundation grants index — 1980. 1981. The Foundation Center, New York.

49. Foundations that send their annual report. 1976. Public Service Materials Center, New York.

50. Fredrickson, D. S. 1979. A history of the recombinant DNA guidelines in the United States. *In* J. Morgan and W. J. Whelan (eds.), Recombinant DNA and Genetic Experimentation, pp. 151–156. Pergamon Press, New York.

51. French, R. D. 1975. Antivivisection and medical science in Victorian society. Princetown University Press, London.

52. Frucht, K. 1977. Art and animal welfare. Animal Reg. Stud. **1**:47–72.

53. Gardner, M. 1978. Aha! insight. Scientific American, New York.

54. Garfield, E. 1983. Introducing *Sci-Mate* — a menu-driven microcomputer software package for online and offline information retrieval. Part 1. The *Sci-Mate Personal Data Manager*. Curr. Contents, no. 12, pp. 5–15.

55. Garfield, E. 1983. Introducing *Sci-Mate* — a menu-driven microcomputer software package for online and offline information retrieval. Part 2. The *Sci-Mate Universal Online Searcher*. Curr. Contents, no. 14, pp. 5–15.

56. Godman, A., and E. M. F. Payne. 1979. Longman dictionary of scientific usage. Longman, New York.

57. Goodrich, J. E. 1977. Historical vignette — the first 100 years of antivivisection — 1824 to 1924. Mayo Clinic Proc. **52**:257–259.

58. The grants register — 1983-1985. 1982. C. A. Lerner and R. Turner (eds.). St. Martin's Press, New York.

59. Guide for the care and use of laboratory animals. 1978. DHEW Publication No. (NIH) 78-23. U.S. Government Printing Office Washington, D.C.

60. Hammett, H. B. 1974. How to write a book review: a guide for students. Soc. Sci. **65**:263–265.

61. Hunt, M. 1982. Research through deception. New York Times Magazine, September 12, pp. 66 and 139–142.

62. Huth, E. J. 1982. How to write and publish papers in the medical sciences. ISI Press, Philadelphia.

63. Index to Scientific Reviews. Institute for Scientific Information, Philadelphia.
64. Jackson, P. W., and S. Messick. 1967. The person, the product, and the response: Conceptual problems in the assessment of creativity. *In* J. Kagan (ed.), Creativity and learning, pp. 1–19. Houghton Mifflin, Boston.
65. Jaynes, J. 1976. The origin of consciousness in the breakdown of the bicameral mind. Houghton Mifflin, Boston.
66. Johansen, I. N. 1976. Write your ticket to success: A do-it-yourself guide to effective resume writing and job hunting. Job Hunter's Forum, Annapolis, Md.
67. Katz, J. 1982. It's time to reverse our retreat from reality in teaching college students. Chron. Higher Educ. **24**(21):40.
68. Keeslar, O. 1982. Financial aids for higher education catalog. W. C. Brown, Dubuque, Iowa.
69. Kemp, J. E. 1980. Planning and producing audiovisual materials, 4th ed. Chandler, Scranton, Pa.
70. Kornfeld, L. L., G. McClung Siegel, and W. L. Siegel. 1981. How to beat the high cost of learning. Rawson, Wade, New York.
71. Kunka, R. L., and A. K. Kunka. 1982. The use of overhead transparencies in pharmacy education. Am. J. Pharm. Educ. **46**:68–70.
72. Lakein, A. 1974. How to get control of your time and your life. Signet, New York.
73. Lang, C. M. 1972. Scheduling animal use by researchers. Lab. Animal, Sept./Oct. pp. 22–24.
74. Lathrop, R. 1977. Who's hiring who, 3rd ed. Ten Speed Press, Berkeley, Calif.
75. Library of Congress — subject headings. 1980. Vols. I and II. Library of Congress, Washington, D.C.
76. Literary Market Place. 1983. Bowker, New York.
77. MacGregor, A. J. 1978. Preparing poster talks. IEEE Trans. Prof. Commun. **PC-21**(3):103–105.
78. MacKenzie, R. A. 1972. The time trap. McGraw-Hill, New York.
79. MacKinnon, D. W. 1962. The nature and nurture of creative talent. Am. Psychol. **17**:484–495.
80. Madsen, D. 1983. Successful dissertations and theses. Jossey-Bass, San Francisco.
81. Maizell, R. E. 1979. How to find chemical information. A guide for practicing chemists, teachers, and students. Wiley, New York.
82. Malinowsky, H. R., and J. M. Richardson. 1980. Science and engineering literature: A guide to current reference sources, 3rd ed. Libraries Unlimited, Rochester, N.Y.
83. Mansfield, R. S., and T. V. Busse. 1981. The psychology of creativity and discovery. Scientists and their work. Nelson-Hall, Chicago.
84. Medawar, P. B. 1979. Advice to a young scientist. Harper and Row, New York.
85. Media review digest. 1979. E. J. Schwartz (ed.). Perian Press, Ann Arbor, Mich.
86. Medical books and serials in print. 1983. Bowker, New York.
87. Mill, J. S. 1891. A sytem of logic, 8th ed. Harper, New York.

88. Miller, W. F., and P. E. Shay. 1982. High technology: management and policy implications and emerging opportunities. Stanford Research Institute, Menlo Park, Calif.

89. Morrison, R. T., and R. L. Boyd. 1973. Organic chemistry, 3rd ed., p. 2. Allyn and Bacon, Boston.

90. Mullins, C. J. 1977. A guide to writing and publishing in the social and behavioral sciences. Wiley, New York.

91. Nalimov, V. V. 1982. Realms of the unconscious: the enchanted frontier. R. G. Colodny (ed.). ISI Press, Philadelphia.

92. National Cancer Institute safety standards for research involving oncogenic viruses. 1975. DHEW Publication No. (NIH) 75-790. U.S. Government Printing Office, Washington, D.C.

93. NIH extramural programs—funding for research and research training. 1983. NIH Publication No. 83-33. National Institutes of Health, Bethesda, Md. Guide to programs—1983. National Science Foundation, Washington, D.C.

94. NIH guidelines for the laboratory use of chemical carcinogens. DHHS Publication No. (NIH) 81-2385. 1981. U.S. Government Printing Office, Washington, D.C.

95. Pais, A. 1982. "Subtle is the Lord . . .": the science and life of Albert Einstein. Oxford University Press, London.

96. Paradis, J. C. 1983. Improving technical communications to improve productivity. Chem. Eng. News **61**(11):31–32.

97. Partridge, E. 1963. Usage and abusage: A guide to good English. Penguin, New York.

98. Pelz, D. C., and F. M. Andrews. 1976. Scientists in organizations. Productive climates for research and development, revised ed. Institute for Social Research, University of Michigan, Ann Arbor.

99. The performance dynamics worldwide directory of job-hunting contacts: A guide to 2400 employment recruiters. Performance Dynamics, Parsippany, N.J.

100. Perrin, P. G., and G. H. Smith. 1955. Handbook of current English. Foresman, Chicago.

101. Personal Filing System (PFS) for Apple II. 1982. Software Publishing Corp., Mountain View, Calif.

102. Postdoctoral appointments and disappointments. 1981. National Academy Press, Washington, D.C.

103. Pratt, D. 1980. Alternatives to pain in experiments on animals. Argus Archives, New York.

104. Proxmire, W. 1980. The fleecing of America. Houghton Mifflin, Boston.

105. Random House dictionary of the English language. 1966. Random House, New York.

106. Reid, E. E. 1961. Invitation to chemical research. Franklin, Palisade, N.J.

107. Report of the AVMA Panel on Euthanasia. 1978. J. Am. Vet. Med. Assoc. **173**:59–72.

108. Rocha e Silva, M. 1982. The rational frontiers of science. Krieger, Malabar, Fla.

109. Roe, A. 1951. A psychological study of eminent biologists. Psychol. Monogr., Vol. 65, No. 331.

110. Roget's university thesaurus. 1981. C. O. S. Mawson (ed.). Barnes & Noble, New York.
111. Roper, F. W., and J. A. Boorkman. 1980. Introduction to reference sources in the health sciences. Medical Library Association, Chicago.
112. Rostow, W. W. 1983. The barbaric counter revolution: cause and cure. University of Texas Press, Austin.
113. Sagan, C. 1977. The dragons of eden. Ballantine Books, New York.
114. Scientific and technical books and serials in print. 1983. Bowker, New York.
115. Sheehan, J. C. 1982. The enchanted ring. The untold story of penicillin. MIT Press, Cambridge, Mass.
116. Slobodkin, L. B. 1971. Scientific sterility in middle age. Am. Sci. **59**:678–679.
117. Smith, R. V. 1980. Development and management of research groups. A guide for university researchers, pp. 68–69. University of Texas Press, Austin.
118. Snell, E. E. 1979. Comment. Discovery – Research and Scholarship at the University of Texas at Austin **4**(2):2–3.
119. Stainton, E. M. 1980. Some pointers on style. Scholarly Publishing **12**:75–88.
120. Stainton, E. M. 1980. The uses of dictionaries. Scholarly Publishing **11**:229–241.
121. Steere, N. V. (ed.). 1971. CRC handbook of laboratory safety, 2nd ed. CRC Press, Boca Raton, Fla.
122. Sternberg, D. 1981. How to complete and survive a doctoral dissertation. St. Martin's Press, New York.
123. Strunk, W., Jr., and E. B. White. 1979. The elements of style, 3rd ed. Macmillan, New York.
124. Sugden, V. M. 1973. The graduate thesis; the complete guide to planning and preparation. Pitman, New York.
125. The synonym finder. 1961. J. I. Rodale (ed.). Rodale Books, Emmaus, Pa.
126. Tax information on scholarships and fellowship grants. Publication 507 (10–70). U.S. Government Printing Office, Washington, D.C.
127. Thomson, W. (Lord Kelvin). 1894. Popular lectures and addresses by Sir William Thomson, 1891–1894. Macmillan, New York.
128. Tichy, H. 1966. Effective writing for engineers, managers, scientists. Wiley, New York.
129. Twedt, D. W. 1977. A marketing strategy for marketing knowledge – or how to publish and prosper. J. Market. **69**(April):69–72.
130. Van Nostrand scientific encyclopedia. 1982. 6th ed. D. M. Considine (ed.). Van Nostrand Reinhold, New York.
131. Watson, J. B. 1914. Behavior: an introduction to comparative psychology. Holt, New York.
132. Weaver, W. 1959. Dither. Science **130**:301.
133. Webster's new collegiate dictionary. 1980. Merriam, Springfield, Mass.
134. Webster's third new international dictionary, unabridged. 1981. The great library of the English language. Merriam, Springfield, Mass.

135. Where America's large foundations make their grants. 1983. 5th ed. J. Dermer (ed.). Public Service Materials Center, New York.

136. White, C. M. 1973. Sources of information in the social sciences: a guide to the literature, 2nd ed. American Library Association, Chicago.

137. White, V. P. 1975. Grants—how to find out about them and what to do next. Plenum Press, New York.

138. Wilder, Thorton, author, dies. 1975. Austin Am. Statesman **62**(134):20, Dec. 8.

139. Zelnio, R. N., J. P. Gagnon, and V. L. Pashion. 1977. BIBLIO: a reprint file algorithm. Am. J. Pharm. Educ. **41**:44–47.

140. Zinsser, W. 1980. On writing well—An informal guide to writing nonfiction, 2nd ed. Harper and Row, New York.

141. Zuckerman, H. A. 1977. Scientific elite; Nobel laureates in the United States. Free Press, New York.

Index